# It's My Church
# and I'll Stay If I Want To

# It's My Church and I'll Stay If I Want To

## Affirming Catholicism

### LONNI COLLINS PRATT

Liguori/Triumph
LIGUORI, MISSOURI

*Imprimi Potest:*
Richard Thibodeau, C.Ss.R.
Provincial, Denver Province
The Redemptorists

Published by Liguori/Triumph
An imprint of Liguori Publications
Liguori, Missouri
www.liguori.org
www.catholicbooksonline.com

Copyright 2003 by Lonni Collins Pratt
ISBN 0-7648-1096-0
Library of Congress Control Number: 2003111287

Printed in the United States of America
07 06 05 04 03   5 4 3 2 1
First edition

*To Harry, Mike, Andy, Tom, Lorri, and Noel:*
*siblings by the will of God,*
*friends in the hard and miraculous moments.*

# Contents

•◆•

# Acknowledgments

•◆•

I would especially like to thank a number of people.
No book is ever the work of any one person. For
much of my writing, I have worked with a collaborator, Daniel Homan, OSB. In those previous books he has
been my partner and co-wrestler of words. Although we did
not write this book together, he has stood beside me as I have
written, cheered for me, listened to me, laughed and cried with
me. His ministry and friendship are integral to the story I tell.

I am grateful to the many people who have communi-
cated with me from all corners of the United States. In addition to all those I have not met, many friends and family
have openly discussed their faith and Catholic experience.
Thank you.

There are a number of priests who have influenced the
writing of this book. Thank you to Father Robert, Father
Dennis, Father John Martin, Father Mike, Father Damien,
and Father Rick.

Words fail to express my gratitude and affection for the
monks of St. Benedict Monastery. They have been mentors
and guides, but also brothers.

A very warm and special thanks to Linda, the best agent
and friend any writer could ask for.

# 1

# You Must
# Go Home Again

•◆•

A few months ago I moved out of an office I had
kept for almost fifteen years. From there, I worked as
a freelance writer and also began a small business.
David, my husband, also has an office in the building. He
too will soon be moving because our local historical society is going to make a museum out of the place. Seems
appropriate. It's a place where my dreams flourished—
and also where my dreams fell broken at my feet. It is a
place where I evolved from one kind of person into another without changing substantially at all. Friendships
formed and faded, some even stayed. Over and over, David
and I fell in love in that place where we often talked, held
hands as we walked down to the local diner for lunch,
and even occasionally shut the door to yell at each other.
Yes, the place is jammed with history.

Life accumulated during those fifteen years. Change, as always, smashed into us relentlessly, like little meteors hurled into our orbit. Not only did life accumulate in that office, books accumulated. An enormous number of books.

Books I picked up when my mind was foggy or my heart broken. It has long been an instinct of mine to reach for a book when I need guidance. When I could not find my way, some quiet wisdom would lift a lamp in the dark room. When I needed to laugh, when I needed to cry, the books helped.

Have you ever tried to hold back tears as you talk to a friend? I did that recently and my friend reached for my hand and said, "Please, let me help you cry those tears." Like a good friend, books have helped me cry the necessary tears, howl at the moon, and laugh until the sun broke through.

The move out of the office marked a passage. After working outside of my home for fifteen years, I was going back. David and I are raising our five-year-old granddaughter, Gina, in a kind of family co-op that keeps her parents involved but means she lives with us. Not only did I want to give more time to nurturing her, I felt driven to simplify our lives. Scaling down to what matters most, this is what was on my mind as I began to sort through thousands of books, files, notebooks, and correspondence.

As I dug into the dusty old books and papers, I looked for whatever pearl of great price was buried there. What were the lessons of the years spent doing what I did in that office? What was worth keeping and taking with me into the next movement of life?

If there was anything to be salvaged from the pile of books in my office, it would be something worth taking from

the old life into the new life. Fifteen yeas ago I had entered
that office newly married, my children were young teenagers.
I was active in my Protestant church, and within that church
there was a core group of friends who supported my life.
Everything had changed. Marriage after fifteen years is different, and my little girls are now grown women. When I
returned to Catholicism I not only lost a successful career
as a writer in the evangelical world, I lost the church that
had been my home and I lost the relationships intwined
within it.

Somehow, all of that was represented in the contents of
my office. I went through shelf after shelf, box after box,
sorting and piling more or less unconsciously. I was not ten-
tative. Clearly, somehow clearly, there were books to keep
and books I could do without. Almost without exception I
made that decision in the two or three seconds that a book
rested in my hand.

Weeks later, I began placing books on the shelves of my
home office. It was a tiny number of books in comparison
to what I'd given up. Some inner wisdom had been at work
while I sorted books. Somehow, I kept the books that had
helped me find my way. Every time I go into that office, I
am surrounded by a cloud of witnesses who have propped
me up, led me to prayer, and sustained me during the worst.
To others, my collection of books might seem pointless, scattered, and maybe even without reason. What I know is that
I am who I am, in part, because of the gentle influence of
those books.

I tell you this story because my experience, with both
the Catholic Church and the Protestant Church, is represented in that collection of books. I am unable to fully rid

myself of either religious experience. I don't even want to. Respect for my own journey kept me from pitching those books. The books are rather like an archaeological dig into the whole of my spiritual journey—relics from the various places I've been, the theologies I've considered, embraced, rejected, and come to terms with. There is a book about prayer, the basics of prayer, that I read at a time when I could not pray. A book about solitude, a book about marriage, a book about loss, a book about change. It is an odd collection of Ray Bradbury and Flannery O'Connor. Philip Yancey and Joan Chittister. Walter Wangerin and Hans Kung. Raymond Brown and C. S. Lewis. Sue Monk Kidd and Richard Rohr.

Even though I no longer agree with everything in some of those books, they are my soul-shaping companions. I honor their presence, we have made a long journey together and we are not yet finished. My gut tells me not to burn bridges behind me, to let an occasional messenger cross the gully of change.

I cannot be anything but Catholic. But I do not regret the years lived differently either. I am uniquely qualified to address the question of why remain Catholic, or return to Catholicism. Why not run for the doors in a time like this?

My eldest daughter, who will soon be thirty, told a friend of hers from high school that I had gone back to Catholicism. The young woman was confused.

"What? Why would she do that?" she wondered out loud. "People leave the Catholic Church, they don't go back to it. Especially with all that is happening now. Your mother is so smart, why would she do a thing like that?"

It's a question we can't avoid.

Why indeed?

How can a thinking person, a person who is concerned with authentic faith, a person who wants to keep the children safe, a person who expects that people behave in accordance with what they claim to be ultimate values—how does that person remain Catholic in times like these?

In *It's My Church and I'll Stay If I Want To,* I don't spend a lot of time wrestling with the critical issues that face today's Church. It doesn't take half a brain to see what's gone wrong. Too much power and not enough accountability. Too much secrecy, not enough prayer. Too many men, not enough women. Splashed across headlines, bellowing from the evening news, and ticking across the screens of the Internet, we have been beaten up with what is wrong with Catholicism.

At this writing there are positive steps being taken, steps that appear to be in the right direction of more lay involvement, more accountability, more sensitivity to the way people have been wounded. We have reason to believe that the issues will be dealt with. I personally have very little faith in the institution or its willingness to change. History has shown us that those who have power are reluctant to surrender it. I do, however, believe this is God's church, instituted of God, birthed by God, nurtured by God—and God has not abandoned us.

In his 1992 book, *Simplicity: The Art of Living,* Franciscan priest, author, and popular retreat speaker Father Richard Rohr writes, "Power is surely not intrinsically wrong, but it is very dangerous and, in my opinion, only spiritually mature people can handle it…. I see nothing in the New Testament that tells me Jesus intended or desired his new community to be modeled on the power structures of the Roman Empire."

We moderns know enough about history to recognize the fault line running through the monolith that is Catholicism. Despite our optimism, born in faith, there's no escaping the hard questions that keep the most faithful of Catholics awake.

So why don't we run for the doors? I suspect that Catholics stay for many of the same reasons that I returned. It comes down to authenticity, to living in my own skin, accepting who I am. I did not remain Protestant because I am Catholic. But I am now Catholic with a big fat history as a Protestant. I have been over the fence; I have come home.

I am not a theologian, I don't teach religion, history, or philosophy. I am not a professed religious. I am a writer and journalist who just happens to be Catholic. I was born Catholic, just as my parents were born Catholic, and their parents were born Catholic.

I left Catholicism at sixteen; at forty, I returned. I spent twenty-four years in other churches, looking for a God to pray to, a God to love and be loved by, a way to be Christian and spiritual. A way to just be. I spent most of that time as an Evangelical Protestant of various Wesleyan stripes, eventually coming to rest in a United Methodist Church where I met my husband and remained active until the day I became Catholic again.

As a young woman, I attended a conservative Bible college. I was a pastor's wife, a youth pastor, a women's minister, Sunday schoolteacher, Christian education minister, and even a softball commissioner. I taught teaching skills to Sunday schoolteachers and conflict management to youth pastors.

I wrote hundreds of articles for Protestant magazines,

contributed to books and devotionals, planned and wrote curriculum. I was called by the a Protestant flagship publication, *Christianity Today*, "…an Evangelical leader." My family and I were featured in *Focus on the Family* and *Guideposts*, both high profile Evangelical magazines. I won several writing awards within the Evangelical religious culture. I was a "frequent contributor" to *Moody Magazine* and *Discipleship Journal*. Not only did I become one of them, I taught them how to be who they are, in the articles I wrote and the retreats, workshops, and seminars I presented.

Let me be clear. I haven't listed these activities to impress. I tell you only for the sake of demonstrating that I was not simply a churchgoing Protestant. I practiced it. Really practiced it.

So, why did I leave the life I so persistently carved out for myself? As I said, authenticity. Recently, an editor for one of the most influential of the Protestant magazines asked me to write an article about why I returned to Catholicism. I tried very hard to write that article, but it simply came down to this. I am Catholic because I am Catholic.

My task has been to choose Catholicism. Not that I object to being genetically Catholic; I don't. I learned a long time ago that one of the ways to peace of mind is to want what you have, rather than focusing on having what you want. To live fully, this life strategy means learning to want, to love what you have; it is no easy thing. I have a Catholic soul, but I am still in the process of learning to embrace it and love it.

Discovering that my soul remained primitively and permanently Catholic did not happen overnight. That story is woven into these pages. There was a process that took several

years. A series of epiphanies in which I seemed to more fully come to my senses. The process did, however, culminate on a certain day, in a certain place—during a specific crisis.

I had been struggling with the kinds of things that people think about at midlife. It is so classic that it is rather dull. The midlife brain and spirit can become lost in the search for what matters most, who am I halfway through this journey, that sort of thing.

David and I were sitting in church one Sunday morning in November, he had not yet become a pastor. Our daughter Andrea was late for church. She was sixteen, almost seventeen. She drove in a separate car that morning because she was picking up a friend for church. As the first song began I turned around looking for her; something felt very wrong.

About ten minutes into the service, someone walked up the side aisle and motioned David and me to follow them. We slipped out quietly. There was a police officer in the lobby of the church. He said our daughter had been in an auto accident and was being airlifted to the hospital. The plan had been to take her to a trauma center about fifty miles away, however they had decided to take her to the local hospital instead—in an attempt to stabilize her condition. Friends told us later that as we left the room, they heard the helicopter over the hospital (it's located across the street from the church).

That night, I sat next to her bed in the intensive care unit. After hours of trying to stabilize her, after a couple attempts to get the helicopter up in an icy drizzle, after the numbing shock and the waiting, she was finally flown to the trauma center where a lengthy surgery stopped the internal bleeding. Rods were also put into her broken femur

bones in both legs. She remained unconscious with a respirator and dozens of tubes and lines hooked to her.

When you sit beside a child's bed waiting for the next blessed breath, there is no energy available for conjuring up anything other than what comes most naturally. Whatever you lean upon, whatever may rise up in you to pray or curse, it will come from the real you. Our facades crumble in the face of the phone call every parent fears: Come quickly, there's been an accident.

A Catholic chaplain put his hand on my shoulder as he whispered the words my mother had whispered over me, the words her mother whispered over her, "Holy Mary, Mother of God...."

It fell like a torrent on a cracked dry river bottom. Mother, oh dearest Mother, who else but you could know what this is like? Mother Mary, get her home to me...you who have held a broken child in your arms...give this one back to me, to all of us, our world needs her laughter, her love...would it cost God so much to open her eyes and send her home to me?

When the prayer was finished, I was firmly on my way home myself. Later, when I asked the chaplain why he had stopped by to see us he showed me where I had designated myself as "Catholic" on the admittance form. I had not identified myself as Catholic in over twenty years.

There had been other hospitals, other times that someone asked for my official declaration of religious affiliation and what I remember of those times is that my first response was "Catholic," but it was a hushed response, one I shoved down and ignored. A hushed inner core of Catholic identity isn't unusual. Even when a person hasn't been to Mass in

twenty or thirty years, if you ask them their religious affiliation, a cradle-Catholic will tell you he or she is Catholic,
and they rarely feel it should be qualified or explained. Nam-
ing myself as Catholic was one of the most honest things I
had done in decades.

There are many lies we tell about ourselves when we are
young. We do it to secure good jobs and to snag the best
mate in the bunch. We do it to keep the clan from isolating
us. We even do it to make peace and maintain stability. We
do our share to keep the boat from rocking. I've heard this
farce of the self likened to a mask; but it's more like a bullet-
proof suit, head-to-toe, than a mask.

Truly, we are probably hiding and hoping the disguise
stays put, but we are hiding because we feel ambushed by
life and love. We feel like we are under fire.

There is a singleness of purpose that happens in middle
life, the compulsion to shed the excess is irresistible. The
body armor becomes just too heavy to lift, too heavy for old
bones to carry, so we shrug off the lies because we are weary,
not because we are better, deeper, or wiser.

I had left Catholicism at sixteen, not because of some
"born-again" experience, not because I thought through the
theology (How many teenagers do you know who have ever
thought through theology) or had a religious revelation. You
see, there was this dark-eyed boy who wasn't Catholic. He
asked me to go to church with him. It mattered to him, he
mattered to me.

I had not been intentional about my Catholicism. I was
also not intentional about becoming Protestant. I was simply very young and head over heels for a cute boy with a
fast car. I married the boy.

I spent most of my young life, including the teenaged marriage, trying to get away from home, rebelling against my family, culture, and religion. How could I know that I would spend the second half of my life trying to find my way home again?

When I needed a way to be a person of faith that would sustain me in the wreckage, I looked over my shoulder and discovered that my Catholic faith had never gone away.

To be Catholic is to live a certain way. This doesn't mean all Catholics are exact duplicates of all other Catholics, or that our lives more or less take the same path. No. Nor is the Catholic life about the trappings; it is about a certain way to be human and to believe. Catholicism, though seemingly bent on fulfilling every dark stereotype ever flung at it, is also a huge, miraculous playground where one minute it's bread and the next it's Jesus. Try that in a Presbyterian church.

A Baptist minister once told me how much he envied Catholics the certainty of Real Presence.

"Real Presence," he mused wistfully. "In my church, people talk about whether or not God is present in a moment, or a certain church service, and there is something hopeful but unconvinced about the way we talk about it. We pray things like 'God, be present with us as we gather to honor you,' silly things like that. At best, we can hope God is present in our attempts to worship. Sometimes I might think I sense God, and my wife will say she didn't feel anything. But, you Catholics always know. Go to church and God shows up. What you feel doesn't matter; God will feed you and love you without exception. Just the thought of Real Presence brings a lump to my throat."

When we sentimentalize anything we cease to see the thing itself and become only more aware of ourselves. There is a danger that in trying to point to what is lasting and hugely good in Catholicism, I will do no more than point to my own sentiment. Instead, to locate the biggest goodness there is in Catholicism, we need to get past sentiment and see the thing itself. This awareness is hard to do when the thing is woven into your being.

My years as a Protestant help me do so, but not without fail. I am hopelessly attached to my Catholicism. I can only write as one who loves the beast. Many years ago, I had a cat named Madison. Madison hunted constantly. When weather allowed me to be outside, he would bring his kills and drop them adoringly at my feet, looking up at me for approval. The day he brought me a still warm baby bunny, I knew I had to do something.

After that, I would make a lot of noise whenever I let him outside—and I let him out much less. While he prowled, I pulled weeds and rustled bushes and stomped around, or sang loudly as I hung sheets out to dry. I never sat out in the sun reading without a radio blasting. If you love a killer, you have a responsibility to clear the area of possible prey. I am not going to lose sight of this reality as I write. While I have not been violated by a priest, I was, at eleven years old, raped by an uncle, my favorite and most trusted uncle.

I am on a first-name basis with that particular monster and I will never make light of the children's suffering. However, I love being Catholic. I am deeply grateful to God that I am Catholic. I am intentionally Catholic. With not quite ten years passed since my return, the infatuation has not yet faded or melted into mellow. So, I am passionate about it.

Going home is always a bit scary. Will it be the same? Will I know the way? Will I be welcome?

In the weeks before taking Eucharist at a Catholic Mass for the first time, I asked a lot of questions. A friend, who was a Benedictine novice at the time, offered to talk to his prior about all my questions.

He said, "If you're going to attend Mass, it will probably be here (at the monastery). Why don't I ask Father Dan if there is any problem with you returning and taking Eucharist?" I agreed. I had been visiting the monastery occasionally for long walks and conversations with the monks. I had even stayed overnight at the retreat house when I needed to be alone. Yes, if there was a safe place to test my wings as I returned, it would be the monastery.

Days later, my friend called and said, "Father Dan said you are more than welcome. He said, 'Tell her she is welcome to come home.'"

His response startled me and I replied, "What? No strings attached?"

He surely smiled as he replied, "My dear friend, Benedictines don't even know how to attach strings."

The words "...she is welcome to come home," haunted me for months.

# 2

# Cigar Peddlers
# and Mystics

•◆•

In the 1995 movie, *Smoke*, Auggie Wren, portrayed by Harvey Keitel, owns a cigar shop in Brooklyn at Third Street and Seventh Avenue. Every day of his much-the-same life, at eight in the morning, Auggie takes a snapshot of his cigar store from the across the street. He calls this project, with its thousands of photos, his "life's work."

Paul (played by William Hurt) is one of the people who goes to the cigar shop to smoke, and to talk. Paul, rather unlike Auggie, is the deep and cultured type. He's a writer who is rigidly blocked. His wife died in brutal, senseless, random street violence. Life isn't making much sense to Paul, and all the angst keeps him from being able to write. Not writing, naturally, is its own sort of torture for a writer. Writing is Paul's life's work.

One day, Auggie shows Paul his "life's work." Paul flips through the pages, countless pages of sameness, countless images of the same spot, collecting one upon another, endlessly. Page after page, picture after picture, of the cigar shop. He keeps flipping the pages, willing to get it, really wanting to get it, but you can see that as the pace at which he's turning the pages increases, his bewilderment deepens. Finally, he says with confusion, "But...they're all the same."

Auggie patiently replies, "You'll never get it if you don't slow down, my friend."

So Paul tries again. He slows down. He begins to notice the tiny distinctions of each photograph, the details of time passing. Sometimes there are people wearing coats, sometimes there is a jogger, or someone on a bike, or a truck making a delivery. There are snapshots of the first snow swirling in the November air. There are times when the soft glow of sunrise turns the neighborhood a mystical pink, times when the size of a garbage truck dwarfs everything.

Like Auggie standing out there on the corner every day with his camera, the spiritual person reads his or her ordinary life. She takes a picture of it, you might say, so that she can spend time with the details, so that she can read it, pray with it, get into it, and find the presence of God that is definitely there—in the details.

What's more, taking a picture of it, paying attention to it, this expresses a conviction that your life is not haphazard. When we strain to see something from a different angle, or in a new light, we are honoring the significance of our lives. When we try to look harder and become intentional about our faith, we honor it and we honor ourselves.

What are we looking for in the snapshot of our Catholicism? We are looking for God among us, watching the movements in the shadows, waiting for the wind to change, hoping for the brush of some strong wing out of the corner of our eyes, looking for the sun to split the clouds. We are looking for clues about the meaning of our lives and, if we have any sense at all, we won't even pretend that being Catholic is anything other than huge. But, it is not the huge institution that defines our lives. Instead, we look closely at one snapshot, one day after another, and in those days we discover the meaning of the whole big thing.

If we squint a bit more, we might even get past the landscape that is littered with our doubts and fear. There is a chance that Something will reveal itself to make clear the significance of our lives. We look for our own stories in the images, we watch to see what has become of us, we look for hints about our futures, and we hope for kind whispers from the past that will, without accusing, tell us the truth about ourselves.

We study our lives so that we recognize what we can count on and what we should have never counted on. We look for patterns, we look for things that connect to other things. This kind of reading is very spiritual work. It challenges us to connect our feelings and memories to places and times and to mine them for whatever is jumping up and down wanting be named.

The word "read" shares a root with words like *art, adorn, ordinary*, and even *ordination*; it means something like "to fit together." This fitting together is what we do when we read our lives, and it is how we become intentional. Most important, you and I listen to our lives because Someone speaks there. Our listening is a response to some call, a response to a voice that elbows us on, beckoning us to get going, to get to the point.

During the months that I struggled with whether or not to return to Catholicism, I also thought a lot about what it means to be called. It isn't that I think we are, each of us, predetermined to be a certain something. I don't think the universe is that rigid. I suspect we can happily and freely use our gifts in a number of ways. My own experience has been that it is not so much what I do with a gift, but that I live in accordance with the way I am gifted—or called. The gift is a call. Could I recognize Catholicism as a gift?

James Hillman, Jungian psychologist, scholar, and author explains a call in a way that has been useful for me, "There is more in a human life than our theories of it allow. Sooner or later something seems to call us onto a particular path. You may remember this 'something' as a signal moment in childhood when an urge out of nowhere, a fascination, a peculiar turn of events struck like an annunciation: This is what I must do, this is what I've got to have. This is who I am." writes Hillman in *The Soul's Code*. He also describes it as "…the feeling that the world wants me here."

I've sensed callings before. It's hard to explain. The desire to return to the Church of my roots felt and sounded in my soul like a calling. My movements toward change were a response to the Voice that has always kept me company. Reading my life, paying attention to it, opens me up to hear God. I realize it's possible to go through life oblivious to God and suddenly experience some sense of calling to something or someone. It just isn't how it has ever happened for me. I have spent many mornings out on the streets trying to get a good picture of my life.

Catholic spirituality is a vision of life on our own corner. It is about seeing better and seeing deeper. This deepening vision doesn't mean that we rise above reality to some state of all-knowing grace. No, spirituality means making peace with the world the way it has been given to us. Rot holes and all. Catholic spirituality doesn't happen in the penthouse of life; rather, its about what happens in our kitchens, bedrooms, and bathrooms.

Author James A. Connor, former Jesuit, gives us a glimpse of how Catholic spirituality works when he wrote about his encounter with a newly snowed-upon night.

I opened the door and got out into the cold. The snow glimmered in the night, as if starlight that had saturated the ground was evaporating into the air. I inhaled deeply and felt the inward pull of my breath, slipping with the rise and fall of it into a more profound state of peace. "Holy, Holy, Holy, / Is the Lord God of Hosts!" I found myself whispering over and over, drawing further into the thickening silence until soon, the head babble of fears, hopes, desires, regrets, depression, elation, stupid ideas, half-formed thoughts, strange hunches all hushed, until I was as quiet inside as the white glowing desert around me, as quiet as the softly pulsing stars....At last I lost all thought of myself...halfway through a single breath, the night revealed itself as joy. The joy did not rise up from me, nor was it me....Joy resonated like a struck bell. It was a presence, something that had been there all along, if only I had been aware.

Aware. This awareness is the difference between being
intentional about my spirituality and just being along for
the ride. Aware of something as ordinary as how God reveals God's wondrous self on a snowy night. It may not be
true in your part of the world, but snow is pretty ordinary
here in Michigan. It's as ordinary as warm oatmeal, a child's
kiss, and the laughter of your best friend. Catholic spirituality is rooted in just such an ordinary.

Come to attention, lift your head, stand up taller and
look closer. In this row upon row, day upon day weaving of
the ordinary, God is present in the Catholic experience. For
Catholic spirituality, attentiveness is the holy challenge, and
the holy effort—to locate God in the sacred happenings of
daily living.

Catholicism does not pretend the ordinary is pretty or
tidy; ours is not a nostalgic or romantic view of day-to-day
living. There is no escaping the messiness of life. This is the
arena where hearts are stomped on and dreams are made
light of; this is the place you can lose your soul, not in the
big mistakes, not in the great evils, but in the ordinary stuff
that happens between dawn and dusk every single day of
your life.

Many years ago, I attended a "Deeper Life" seminar. The
purpose of the event was to help Protestant church leaders
sustain and nurture a spirituality that would get them
through the tough times in ministry. Not a bad goal.

What I noticed, mostly, that day was all the talk about
"going apart," not allowing life to distract you from God,
setting aside time to pray, read the Bible, and study "regardless of what is happening in your life." There was nothing
subtle about the message. Life is an obstacle to getting to

God. It must be overcome if you are going to be closer to God. What you do in your secular moments you must do, but don't let it become more important than what you do in your sacred moments.

As a Catholic, the notion that there is anything about life that keeps me from God is just, well, absurd. Sure, it's a good thing to have time set aside for prayer. May we all do just that more often, but God is not more present at that time than when you're working, watching television, or holding a kid's head over the toilet while he throws up. Our lives are held together by the glue of God in all the gloriously average things we do. Clip your coupons, drink your coffee, go bowling—it will not keep you from God. Better yet, *expect* to find God at the bowling alley.

Obviously, this day after day of the ordinary is not the whole of spirituality. When we talk of being more intentionally Catholic we can't ignore the need for deep solitudes and the ability to reflect and pray. I'm strongly influenced by monastic spirituality, I do not need convincing that contemplation is important. We have to tread carefully though. This search for a contemplative spirituality is the region where religion can develop into neurosis, where introspection can become selfishness. We all know that grandiose ideas about your own spirituality can take you in all sorts of weird directions, and even into some very tragic ones.

Catholicism helps us avoid this trap by keeping us grounded in the ordinary, yet encouraging us to grow into the mystical experience.

There is definitely a place for solitude, there is a time to know yourself and go a bit deeper. Great, go looking for God at the retreat house, the cathedral, or the monastery.

But you must also mow the grass, visit your brother, bake a meat loaf, have a beer with your neighbor, and go to the city council meeting. These are not tasks that we have to accomplish before getting on to the important stuff. This is it!

Look no farther; God is perched in this very moment when you are pouring the cornflakes and dreading the commute to work. If you can't find God here, chances are, you won't find God at the cathedral either.

Catholicism is the mother of a mystical tradition that permeates our Catholic history. Mysticism and contemplation, considered by many to be the deep rivers of spirituality, are among the most misunderstood and misapplied words in a spiritual vocabulary. Mysticism, we've erroneously believed, does not happen in an ordinary life. Mysticism is the realm of whirling visions, angelic voices, and ecstatic states reserved for a very few. No. Wrong. Mysticism is the experience of God that catches your breath, charges your senses, and leaves you with a profound knowing of God's love. The Catholic invitation to mysticism is an invitation to know God and be known by God, in the here and now.

In a book published in 1963, Thomas Merton wrote, "Why do we think of infused contemplation, mystical prayer, as something essentially strange and esoteric, reserved for a small class of almost unnatural beings and prohibited to anyone else? Infused contemplation is…intimately connected with the pure and perfect love of God which is God's greatest gift to the soul. Therefore, if anyone should ask: 'Who may desire this gift and pray for it?'—the answer is obvious: everybody."

The reason we need mysticism, well, that's pretty basic.

The agendas we set for lives jammed with goals, focusing tightly on achievements—these are going to fail at giving us anything like peace of mind. In fact, they seem almost destined to drive us deeper into ourselves, frustrating us to the point of becoming half nuts with wanting that elusive Something More that runs through it all.

Life compels us to become mystics. The need for it is dropped into our souls at the very beginning of whatever a beginning might be. Mysticism is what happens when Love pins you in place for a sliver of time. It can happen anywhere, to anyone, even a monk. The mystical state occurs when we live with a deeper awareness of God's love and presence charging every spinning atom.

The mystic is the person who experiences life as a gift; he doesn't just make noises about it, she doesn't just know that she should experience life as a gift. The other day a priest was telling about a woman he knows, a woman he said has "the heart of a mystic." He said she is one of the most joy-filled people he's ever known despite the deep wells of tragedy that have pitted her life.

"The kinds of things that would crush most of us," he said. Once, he asked her how she kept her peace of mind and held on to her joy.

She replied, "I don't keep a hold on peace or joy, Father; it keeps a hold on me." She is one of the ordinary mystics who has discovered how completely God overtakes our lives.

I had a conversation with a friend that I will never forget. She had stopped by my office for our usual bit of morning bantering and conversation over coffee. Somehow, she started talking about how some people seemed "contented in their ordinariness." Then she said, "You and I aren't like that, we are not the kind of people who will ever settle for ordinary." I replied that I think of myself as very ordinary, and I consider the ordinary an extraordinary thing. She looked confused and repeated, "No, you aren't ordinary."

She's wrong, of course; we are both wonderfully ordinary. We live in a small town, we have regular families, we eat the same sorts of food our neighbors eat, we shop at the same stores, we worry about our children and our parents, we wonder about the future—all very ordinary stuff.

My friend is a successful businesswoman who carries a rosary in her pocket to remind her, as she says, "…that I am not the center of the universe." I think that's a remarkable thing to do. How many other people do I know who do a thing like that? But, it is also very ordinary; it involves nothing more than one woman who picks up a rosary off her dresser every morning of her life and stuffs it into the pocket of her blazer or trousers. Anyone could do it—that makes it ordinary.

A reporter told me about an interview she conducted with a monk, many years ago, when she was still a young reporter. She was influenced and fascinated by the writings of Thomas Merton and all things mystical and/or monastic. Monasticism seemed to her the pinnacle of mystical spirituality. She had been so excited to get an interview with a lifelong monk at a monastery not too far from her own home. Her assignment was to interview the monk about a new retreat program at the monastery.

Fine, but she really wanted the monk to tell her about his mystical tradition and his mystical experiences and all of that stuff that must go with being a very mystical monk. She asked all of the right questions to get information on the program and was satisfied when her "official" assignment was out of the way. Then she really got down to it. She asked him to describe the monastic life. He said something about it being very ordinary. She asked what made the monk different and he replied that nothing made him different.

Well, she knew better than that. She dug in her heels.

What mystical experience of God did the monk have that others could learn from? He shrugged his shoulders, "We pray often," he replied. She said it was more of a question than a response. He tried to steer conversation back to the retreat program. She would have none of it. She asked him to define the mystical experience. She says he leaned back, sort of shook his head a couple times as if trying to rattle some memory loose, and then said, "No, you don't understand, Miss, we're just ordinary monks doing regular sorts of things. We've never come up with a description of mysticism. I could suggest a book...."

Finally, in complete frustration, she leaned close to him and said between gritted teeth, "Well, if you're so damned ordinary, why is everyone infatuated with monasticism?" She remembers he looked into her eyes for a moment and, as a smile grew on his face, he replied, "I don't know—we make fruitcakes?"

Monasticism is fundamentally Catholic. To some it represents the mystical tradition and an ultimate withdrawal to interior places of deep spirit. This interior withdrawal might appear to be contrary to a spirituality that embraces ordinariness. I am very close to a monastic community and have collaborated on several books with a Benedictine monk. In this ten-year relationship with the monastery, the most striking thing about the monks has been how delightfully ordinary those guys are—and how they relentlessly allow the vehicle of the ordinary to take them deeper.

Not too long ago, I arrived at the monastery to claim the guest room that had been prepared for me and found a young monk, Brother Gregory David, scouring the corners of the bathroom floor. The tile is older and, as you'd expect, a bit yellow and stained. Even though it was clean, the staining would not do. A guest, a beloved friend of the monastery, was arriving and the room would be as perfect as he could make it. Scouring corners and dusting shelves in the closet, these are very ordinary tasks, but the monk used the opportunity to express a monastic conviction about guests—that in the guest, you receive Christ. That day, in that moment, he expressed his spirituality in the preparation of a guest room.

I wonder if one of the reasons so many people are trampling down the monastic way is because they hope to avoid the ordinary. Perhaps God inches in a little too close in the ordinary. One or two close calls might send anyone to a monastery in search of a God who is a bit less real than the one you find in the tangle of human relationships.

If you're looking for an ethereal kind of spirituality, I suggest you avoid monasteries completely. There is no floaty aqua God who is all mystery hovering in the ceilings and walls of the monastery. There is only God. The one you find in your own fears and nasty reactions to the annoying monk across the hallway from you, or the God who insists you now take your turn scrubbing toilets and shoveling cow shit.

The monastic God is earthy, practical, and relentlessly insistent that you engage with life. It is here that the best of Catholic earthiness is honored, here where men and women try to live with an ever-increasing sense of God's presence.

The monk has been trained to perceive all of life as holy ground. Yes, his chapel and choir stall is a holy place, and his room makes it possible for him to commune with God alone. In the middle of the Great Silence of the monastic night, he has even heard God sing the stars bright; but the holiest moment of all is when he looks into the eyes of the most annoying of his brothers and says, "Pass the butter, please."

Monastics are men and women who spend every day of their lives looking for God, being found by God, and helping someone else catch a glimpse of God. Monks bicker with one another over the sticky rice and who took the last helping of lemon pudding. Sometimes jealousy and manipulation stick out a foot and trip a monk or two. There are raging resentments, passions, fears, dreams, and disillusionments in a monastery. The biggest difference I discovered between me and the monk is that the monk *expects* to find God in the mess. Me? I still tend to be startled when I discover God up to his elbows in the rot I've made of my life.

The other day, as I read Psalm 139, I was startled again by something I wrote just after my daughter's accident. It was there in the pages of an old prayer book.

"The psalmist is not making a theological observation," I wrote, "or telling of a profound spiritual truth; it is the song of a startled heart that has flown to the ends of the earth, a heart that has made a bed in hell and has drawn the darkness over her head only to discover that God shows up because nothing and no one is beyond God. This is the laughing, weeping song of the person who discovered themselves found when they were sure they were lost. It is the baffled song of a soul humbled by their own devices, delighted to be busted by a relentless God who just doesn't let go—a

God who will find you no matter if the ordinary snatches your last breath."

In dialog with the lines of the psalm I had written more, I had told the secret of the awful dark depression that had cornered me.

## MEDITATION ON PSALM 139

*O God, you have searched me*
*and known me.*
*You know when I sit down*
*and when I rise up.*
*You discern my thoughts from far away.*
*You search out my path and my lying down.*
*Even before a word is on my tongue, O Lord,*
*you know it completely.*
*You hem me in, behind and before,*
*and lay your hand upon me.*
*Such knowledge is too wonderful for me;*
*it is so high that I cannot attain it.*
*Where can I go hide from your spirit?*
*Or where can I flee from your presence?*
*If I ascend to heaven, you are there;*
*if I make my bed in Sheol, you are there.*
*If I take the wings of the morning*
*and settle at the farthest limits of the sea,*
*even there your hand shall lead me,*
*and your right hand shall hold me fast.*
*If I say, "Surely the darkness shall cover me,*
*and the light around me become night,"*
*even the darkness is not dark to you;*
*the night is as bright as the day;*

*for darkness is as light to you....*
*O God, you have searched me*
*and known me.*

> We have a history, You and I.
> There is no one who knew enough to find me here,
> but you did.

*You know when I sit down*
*and when I rise up.*
*You discern my thoughts from far away.*
*You search out my path and my lying down.*

> You know that I have laid down
> more often than risen up,
> that I have made my bed in the wrong places;
> I have taken paths better left un-walked
> and to this place I have come
> to lie down one final time,
> certain that purpose, goodness, and love
> have finally run out for me.
> Convinced to the heart of me
> that all would be better
> with my lying down and final breath.

*Even before a word is on my tongue, O Lord,*
*you know it completely.*
*You hem me in, behind and before,*
*and lay your hand upon me.*
*Such knowledge is too wonderful for me;*
*It is so high that I cannot attain it.*

And so here I am,
where I've made a bed in hell
and put the bottle of pills on the night table
and wrote the good-bye notes,
and then you just show up,
you corner me in even this place
where most people would fear to come after me,
and you take hold of me.

*Where can I go from your spirit?*
*Or where can I flee from your presence?*

If I can't get away from you here,
tell me, is there anywhere you won't come after me?
Does it even matter to you
that all of this mess is my own doing?
Are you so shameless in loving
that you will come after someone like me?

*If I ascend to heaven, you are there;*
*if I make my bed in Sheol, you are there.*
*If I take the wings of the morning*
*and settle at the farthest limits of the sea,*
*even there your hand shall lead me,*
*and your right hand shall hold me fast.*

We both know that I have run
as far, as hard, as I can run
and now I discover that even in my running
you have been leading me to a place
where I will finally feel small enough
to let you lead me home,
rather than trying to build my own kingdom.

*If I say, "Surely the darkness shall cover me,*
*and the light around me become night,"*
*even the darkness is not dark to you;*
*the night is as bright as the day;*
*for darkness is as light to you....*

> Is the darkness in me
> not at all terrifying for you?
> So be it.
> You have found me again.
> I don't know how to run
> from that kind of love.
> I have come to the end
> of myself and my devices;
> I have buried the last dream
> and yet I am still with you, even here.
> So here is my hand,
> get me off this damned ledge
> and take me home.

The ordinary is not always simple, is it? Pain, that's ordinary. Betrayal. Loss. They stomp the life out of us, but they are so ordinary.

•◆•

I don't always want to look for God in the ordinary. I've noticed though that what I *really* don't want to do is locate God in the ordinary stuff. If this happens, my excuses for boredom and laziness fail. It is in the rough and tumble of my own life that God is going to find me. If I, at a sane and sensible place, want to avoid being consumed by this fire that is God, I must make an effort to pay as little attention as possible to my daily living. If I hope to avoid God, I dare not join Auggie out on the corner taking snapshots every day.

Catholic spirituality forbids me to ignore my life. In an almost overwhelming abundance of sacramentals and symbols, Catholicism has convinced my timid heart that God comes to me not only at the Communion table, but in the tables of my friends; not only in the sacrament of reconciliation but in my pale attempts to forgive and be forgiven. The symbolism inherent in Catholicism provides me with a means, a path, to living fully.

One of my favorite Catholic memories is the annual blessing of throats, a sacramental that happens on, or about, February 3, the feast of Saint Blaise, who on his way to being martyred, saw a little boy choking on a fish bone, stopped, and touched the boy's throat, dislodging the bone and saving the child's life.

As you might expect in Michigan, in February, there were always more than a few colds and sore throats present. More than once I went forward to have the candles crossed over my head and laid on my throat while I had a scratchy throat. But, I also knew that it was not about protection from a virus; the annual blessing was not like a flu shot. This was a reminder of God's involvement in all of my life. God cared about my throat, not just my health, but about what I said, what I sang, what I yelled, what I ate and drank.

I was a grown woman, and Protestant, when my grandmother came down with throat cancer. She was eighty-eight years old. She lived to be ninety-eight. Twice in those ten years doctors removed tumors from her throat. She underwent some radiation and chemotherapy, but she was never one to keep going back because the treatment was more likely to kill you than the illness. She always claimed that throat cancer didn't stand a chance because of the yearly blessing of throats. Who knows?

Before the ashes of death are rubbed into our skin on a gray late winter Wednesday, the blessing of throats reminds us that God does not abandon us. Ash Wednesday summons us to the edge of our graves, but not before the blessing of throats reminds us that our very breath is to be celebrated. Both spiritual truths are conveyed to the Catholic heart through the signs and symbols we confront year after year.

Psychologists have a term for how symbols work on us; they call it "afterimage," referring to the image your eye sees after a bright flashing light. Even when the light fades, the image is still with you. The experience of an afterimage is one that any of us who ever had our photo taken or looked into the bright sun can recall. Catholicism leaves us with a permanent afterimage.

And so, lighting a candle does not just set a mood and disperse a fragrance; it welcomes the Christ who is among us. The fragrance is a reminder that we live our lives in the permeating presence of God. When you start the day with the hum of a shower, it is also a call to remember your baptism. Every drop of water ever splashed on me seems to remind me to remember.

Last summer, I spent a lot of time at the beach with my two granddaughters Chelsea and Gina. Chelsea was not quite three years old, Gina was four. The water level of the Great Lakes is currently in a low cycle, so the little ones could play safely, but under my watchful eye, in water that hardly covered their legs. One day, a distant storm moving our way whipped up the waves. Along with visiting friends, I was in the water with the girls.

They loved the higher waves. They dived into them and rode them to the shore. When they went under, they came up sputtering and giggling. We were never far from them, but the girls hardly noticed us; they were abandoned to the waters.

That's how I hope they live their lives, abandoned to the call of their baptisms, lost in the waters of love, able to play and laugh even as the clouds roll toward them. I did not stand in the water and conjure up spiritual thoughts. The children, the water, the waves—it all connected to a symbolism that is in my bones. Catholic symbolism informs the whole of my life.

By memorization and instruction, the nuns and other teachers taught me the Apostles' Creed, the Our Father, and various rituals. My grandmother had a copy of *Goffines' Devout Instructions* (1896 edition). Her mother gave it to her. It is now mine. Prayers from it are burned into my memory and come to me at the oddest times.

During Advent this year, a friend called to ask me to lunch. Such an ordinary thing to do, right? Then she said, "We haven't visited in a while…" and immediately these words from Goffines' sprang into my head (this prayer is from Advent):

We beseech Thee, O Lord, mercifully incline Thine ear unto our prayers, and enlighten the darkness of our minds by the grace of Thy heavenly visitation.

This is an example of rote memorization at work. Catholic symbolism does not work in the same fashion. Instead, it seeps into a person quietly, relentlessly, and permanently while we are occupied learning what to do with a rosary (other than wrap it prettily around little fingers). What you and I did not understand as children was that on one of those nights when sleep won't come, and the heart has forgotten how to pray because noise and foolishness have taken it captive, you can wrap your fingers around that rosary and peace will get you.

Whatever it is in Catholicism that taught me how to internalize, a certain sacramental system was at work in ways I can barely name. I did not learn it in any typical sense of the word. Many Protestants speak of how the Bible comforts and strengthens them. I spent more than two decades studying Scripture and, I hope, letting Scripture study me. There is definitely comfort in those pages and, as the words on the pages transfer into the depths of a person, peace becomes more available, at least that is how it has seemed to me.

Just recently, I had a heated conversation with a friend on the phone. I think he's making some big mistakes; he thinks I don't understand. Our talking never became ugly or judgmental, but it was quite intense. My hands were shaking as I hung up the phone. On the bookshelf next to my desk is a family Bible; you know, one of those barge-sized volumes that stay in families for decade after decade. I ran my hand over it and felt my pulse slow. I took a deep breath. The power of the symbol collected me.

We can say many things about what the Bible is and isn't, about what it means and attempts to mean. At that moment it cleared my vision, it emptied the junk out of a cluttered mind so that I remembered to remember. It was the sum total of peace that has been spoken to me in the words of Scripture, that's what gathered me up peacefully and helped me breathe again. And I did not open the book. The book, the actual bound book published one hundred years ago, it has no power at all; it is a symbol of something else.

I did not learn among my Protestant brothers and sisters that there is a symbolic power in the printed book, a power that holds at the center. Speaking of the book as "symbolic" will, in fact, get you into a terrible lot of trouble among some Protestants.

This notion that the things I touch, the things I eat and drink, the people who kiss me, the wind in my face, bears some mysterious resemblance to God was trickled into my consciousness without my knowing of it. I can put catechism lessons from my mind; this other, I do not know how to make it stop. It is the legacy of Catholicism—the ability to draw the life of God from whatever symbol is at hand has served me well.

We human beings have an inherent longing for God. Scattered around my world are keepers of this longing, little triggers that respond to my yearning by sweeping the veil from strained eyes. Without a way to recognize God among us, my inherent desire for God would be mostly frustrating. Instead, I have learned as a Catholic Christian that the world will respond to my desire for God.

We all go through periods when God is mostly absent, and the absence bends us to the ground. It was that way for me last year during Lent. It was the third week of Lent and I only hoped that what seemed like a spiritual desert would end soon. I went to Mass on Saturday night because there would be fewer people.

I liked the boyish-looking, fortysomething-year-old priest, Father Dennis, a former cop with keen street smarts and a gentleness that takes your heart right away. As much as I liked him, which was almost immediately, the parish has not felt particularly Catholic. Walking into a Catholic church is not liking walking into any other place on the planet. That's how it's been for me. This particular parish didn't have much religious art, the stained-glass windows were nothing to write home about, they had chairs rather than pews, the crucifix was placed to the side, almost as if they were a bit ashamed of it. It felt more like a pole barn than a Catholic church.

I admit it. I like statues, organ music, and breathtaking art. I like incense and vigil candles. I like mosaics. I want the stations of the cross on the walls all the way around the church, and I am quite fond of kneelers, even though I stand when some other Catholics think I should be kneeling. I like Latin splattered here and there. The symbols call me home and then send me out stronger.

The single most annoying thing about the parish decor, despite the gifted, likable priest, is the floating Jesus doll. It is suspended over the altar, arms outstretched, feet appropriately together. On its molded plastic face is a dumb Mona Lisa look. It reminds me of the inflatable Jesus and angel dolls that I've seen in the aisles of various religious goods trade shows.

As I entered, I dipped my fingers into the fountain where holy water would usually flow. Sand. Welcome to Lent. As if I needed a reminder that my heart was dried up and ready to be blown away by the first moderate breeze. I found a seat on the aisle and glanced up. Thank God, the dreadful Jesus doll was draped with purple cloth for Lent. I would not have to spend the evening under its goofy gaze.

I wasn't seated very long when Father Dennis came over to welcome me. Here and there parishioners hugged, chatted, and smiled at one another—noisily. I'm accustomed to quiet when I enter the monastery chapel. In most other Catholic churches, there is a welcoming silence rather than all that chatter. For all the gleeful greeting and conversations, handshaking, and backslapping it might as well have been a Methodist church. I clenched my teeth and silently grumbled at God. Wouldn't you know it—the Scripture text was about the grumbling Israelites. Father Dennis began his homily by reminding us that we human beings are grumblers. Busted.

It was March, women's history month. I don't know if that accounted for all the women who assisted during Eucharist. The church is in the Saginaw Diocese of Michigan where we are blessed to have Kenneth Untener as bishop. He was one of the first American bishops to publicly discuss the ordination of women.

The woman who put the Body of Christ into my hand was probably seventy years old. She stood very straight, her eyes were bright, the lights glistened in her thick silvery hair as she said, "The Body of Christ."

I wonder if she ever expected to hold the host in her hand, I wonder if she ever dreamed of such a thing. There she was, standing beside the priest. When all of us had received, she served the boy-faced priest the cup. I watched her lips move as she said, "The Blood of Christ." Then he accepted the cup from the hands of a woman. It was a breathless moment.

Accompanying the older woman and priest at the altar were a young boy, of ten or so, and another woman, Patty. We learned later that it was her forty-seventh birthday. The woman was, well, different. She is beautiful just the way God made her, but also unlike any other woman in the room. She had Downs syndrome. I watched her take the bread and give it, watched her face light up as people smiled at her. Watched her standing right under that annoying Jesus doll with pierced feet pointing right down at her.

There was something very holy about the unlikely foursome beneath the clownish Christ hiding in his Lenten purple. The Christ was still there, even if he was covered, dangling in the air between earth and heaven over such a sacred romp as the one that was happening up there at the altar that chilly March night.

After Eucharist, the priest, attired in his dazzling purple robes threaded with gold, told us it was Patty's birthday. He called her to join him again. We all sang happy birthday as he tucked the little woman under his arm. Those back-slapping people cried. I cried. We were caught up in some spectacle of Love beyond us. The priest lifted his cherub face as he sang. He looked like he'd laugh out loud, cherub face or not. This is one clever guy. There we were, God's own bumbling, glorious bunch, singing happy birthday at the end of Mass. Nestled against the priest's side, Patty grinned and wept, her feet wiggled as if she could hardly contain the dancing in them. I swear even the toes of the Jesus doll wiggled with the insidious joy of the moment.

That's all of us up there tucked under God's arm, I

thought. All of us misfits, broken and coming apart, belonging to one another, lovingly held to God's side. Father Dennis, he's the official representative of Christ, that's what the hierarchy says. But I can tell you that Patty personifies Christ too and so did the little boy and the old woman and even those people who would loosen your elbow with all that handshaking. All of us together living our lives under the gaze of a Christ who seems more clown than prophet in times like these, we find ourselves being the presence of God to one another, like it or not.

I doubt that Patty was thinking of how she became all of us tucked under God's arm. She was just being Patty and enjoying her birthday, enjoying the love of the people who go to church with her. By her presence, we all felt this great big shattering love drop on our heads, such a weight of love it should have crushed us, but it didn't. It healed us way down deep. We were all more alive and more human because of it.

As we left, the priest said, "Watch out for one another!" and I remembered my mother telling us kids to take care of one another and look after one another. "You're family," she'd remind us as we left for school, "all you have is each other." The priest in his purple dress was not only like God holding us under his wing, he was like a mother sending her babies out into the world one more time.

I had this same feeling recently. I had coffee one morning with another priest in the Diocese of Saginaw. We spent a couple hours together on a frigid January morning, with the wind blasting from Lake Huron only a block from the rectory. When we were finished, he walked me to the door.

I put on my coat and gloves, then reached for the door

handle and he said, "Please…zip up your coat. It's so cold out there…" and his instincts kicked into gear. I saw his hand twitch, almost reaching for my zipper as if I were six years old. I caught his eye and smiled. He chuckled. I zipped up. He hugged me soundly and sent me off into the cold under his watchful eye, standing there in the cold doorway until I pulled out of his driveway.

Every now and then in this Catholicism I love, some priest has become Christ for me. It catches me off guard every time. I remember the first time it happened. It was only a few weeks after returning to Catholicism.

I was helping on a teen retreat that offers reconciliation on Saturday night. With the lights lowered in the retreat house and music playing, each teen, and the adults too, were invited to leave the general gathering area, walk across a kind of skywalk and go to the priest for reconciliation. The last time I had participated in anything like it, we called it confession. Back then there were heavy dark curtains, sliding screens, whispers—all of it very shame-inducing.

Each of us had written our sins down during a time of reflection. We were also expected to verbally confess. After a dozen or so teens and adults had made the journey across the skywalk and back I rose, trembling, clutching my paper in hand and walked in the candlelight toward the priest.

I knew this man, this monk, this priest. He was not a stranger behind a screen. He was my friend, he cared about me. Maybe that is how he so easily became an icon of Jesus. The most meaningful image of Jesus, for me, is that of Friend.

I handed him the paper and tried to speak but found myself voiceless as I choked on the lump in my throat. He reached for my hands, holding tight while I found my voice.

When I finished, he lay his hand on my head in absolution, then he lifted the paper with the words admitting to the worst of me, and set a match to it. I laughed right out loud. Something lifted, something was left behind, something new dropped on my heart. He grinned.

Inherent in our friendship, and in his role as priest, is the authority to forgive. Unless I believed this, the rite would be empty. But this belief is something life has taught me. I sin against God, but I accomplish this sinning in the ways I sin against people, the ways I sin against love. God understands and forgives without exception—God as he comes to me as friend, spouse, lover; I need this kind of forgiving too. I need a human hand to hold mine, a human tear that is shed over my pain, a human smile that affirms all is well. There is power in the priest who absolves as an icon of God— and as a human being.

I walked the skywalk back to the gathering, hearing the words of Jesus ringing throughout the centuries, "Friend, your sins are forgiven."

The sacraments are inherent to Catholic spirituality. We are not merely fulfilling some requirement in the sacraments, we are being converted, we are growing. God gives life to us in the sacraments. They are not symbols of grace, they are the givers of grace. If there were nothing more than symbolical meaning to the sacraments, like confession, I could not be really changed by it, I could only accept the token of change.

We come away from our sacramental participation softer around the edges. We come away more human. We come away stronger.

# 3

# A Great Big Yes

•◆•

C risis causes change. When I look at my own patterns of change I am hard-pressed to find an instance of personal transformation that happened any other way. Physics teaches us this lesson scientifically. New matter always emerges from the ruins of the old. It is the old, dissolving matter that gives its energy to the new emerging matter. The old does not sink into nothingness, it becomes part of the new.

The atoms of your body contain the great catastrophic and glorious events of the history of all humanity. The air you breathe contains particles that were part of the physical body of Jesus Christ, Mother Teresa, and Hitler. We bear within us not only our own failings and greatness, we hold within us the greatness and lostness that belongs to all of us. Good Friday and Easter are the Christian remembrance of this reality. Each eucharistic celebration remembers that life comes from death.

Easter arrives with the message that death has no staying power. Hold on to your seat—you haven't seen anything
yet. Saint Paul paraphrases the Old Testament prophet Hosea
when he writes: "Where, O death, is your victory? Where,
O death, is your sting?" Hear that? That's the sound a tired
old man who has been beaten, rejected, misunderstood, and
with his last breath he is sticking his tongue out at death.
He knows it's far from over.

There's an old Christmas television special about Rudolph
and one of Santa's helpers who aspires to dentistry. Rudolph
and the elf dentist-wanna-be trudge out into the cold world
feeling like misfits. With a few "misfit" friends, the pair encounter various adversities including a fang-endowed abomi-
nable snowman with a nasty attitude. There is no escaping
the jaws of the ill-tempered beast. Heroically, the little elf
goes over a cliff taking the fanged brute with him to a snowy
death and saves his friends. Sadly, Rudolph and the little
ragtag group head home to Santa's castle.

But, that's not the end of the story. In a blaze of glory,
the elf shows up on Christmas Eve at Santa's door waving
his dentist's pliers and riding the now-toothless beast, made
harmless by the little misfit.

This is what Jesus has shown us about death: it has no
teeth. It bites, but the bite, that we will someday know,
amounts to nothing. Dreams die, relationships die, people
die—when it happens, remember death has no sting left; it's
a wasp without a stinger. Just another ugly pest.

So it is in our lives. We suffer through many deaths before the final one shuts down our ragged hearts. Our coming back to life after these deaths, this is the best reminder
we have that death is not the final word.

We probably accept this reality in our minds, and we hope for it in our hearts. But it doesn't stop the changes brought on by catastrophe from cutting deeply into our lives. We can't simply paint a pretty facade on it and deny the hurting. Maybe the best we can do is to remain with the hurting until whatever is new begins to stir in the rubble at our feet.

It is not unusual that crisis launches us into spiritual change and renewal. During the fourteenth century, a period of warring popes and corruption in high places, a scruffy Italian woman we now call Saint Catherine of Siena lived. There was an unparalleled eruption of mysticism among average people like you and me during this time. Mysticism flourished as the institutional Church splintered apart. Catherine was not a nun; she was a lay Dominican, an oblate of sorts, who advised popes.

When the papacy went into French exile, leaving Rome, it was Catherine who convinced Pope Gregory XI to return to Italy. When religious systems can't find their way home, it is the laity who often point the way. The strength of the laity, if history shows us anything, tends to emerge in a crisis. It isn't that God causes a crisis so we will rise up to our full identities as Christians. God is not the originator of our chaos; God speaks light and order to our chaos, and something new is born. Creation shows us that God does not leave us alone in the darkness of our self-made messes.

Too often, in Catholicism, we have not trusted the wisdom of the lay experience. Laity are left to our complacency. We need our priests for sacramental reasons and for Mass, but most people who have spoken to me about their priests indicate that they have very little to do with their lives. They seem almost peripheral until it's time for a funeral or wedding. The priest does the holy things and the laity don't—it's that reality for many Catholics.

When I was growing up Catholic, I knew very little about the roles of priests, bishops, cardinals…they seemed to have all the answers, certainly they knew more than I did. Overall, it's not a bad way for a child of fourteen to approach her spirituality: learn from those who know more, have lived more than she has.

However, I am no longer a child. Where adults once made choices for me, I now make my own choices. My parents raised me in the Catholic faith—but at some point it must become my intentional choice to be Catholic. This is true even thought I've learned that it's nearly impossible to stop being Catholic. Maturity requires that I take possession of it, that I put on the robes of my faith with these adult hands of mine—especially when it gets tough.

Vatican II did not simply present an open door for lay Catholics to become more active and informed. It compelled us to do so. Vatican II is not only about modernizing Catholicism or making it more culturally relevant. Important things these. But, Vatican II is about reform, change, transformation. It is about a new direction, a new way of being Catholic that we have yet to take hold of fully. Every single Catholic is obligated to shape and follow a carefully and authentically informed Christian conscience. Does this mean that anything goes? Of course not, that's just silly. It is not a license to dissent on the basis of "gut" feelings and what is convenient or not convenient.

When you and I have prayerfully, carefully, and honestly drawn an informed conclusion, we must live and act according to that conviction. Catholics must not obey, even an official teaching of our beloved Church, in violation of personal conscience. If you want a life that is spread heavy with the scent of misery, just live in violation of your own deepest convictions. It will destroy you every time.

After decades of being Christian, I have come to the careful conclusion that my conscience must be based on a simple, yet foundational, premise. What did Jesus teach? Forgive the cliché, what would Jesus do?

Do I require the Catholic Church to instruct me in what Jesus would teach and do? Certainly I require some instruction as a young person, or a person new to the faith. I must study Catholic theologians and Catholic dogma. I must conjure up the courage to dive into the Scriptures on my own. I must not dismiss the official teachings of the Church.

Ultimately, though, it is the life and teachings of Jesus that shape my spirituality. I have spent my adult life loving this Lord of Life, chasing him down in all the places he can be found, learning his words and trying to get those words into my own heart. I don't have all the answers, but my education, my effort, my very best intention, means that I am immensely capable of finding answers and being open to the Holy Spirit. Not only am I capable of forming my own conclusions, I must be adult enough to do so.

Growing up in the decade before Vatican II, there was a Catholic Church that I thought I knew. This was, in my own mind, the Church I would be returning to. I left before Vatican II took hold in my little parish. The Church I knew was fixed, rooted to the universe. Immovable.

And then—like our concepts of purgatory and hell—our idea of Church moved as well.

Reform was then, and is now, imperative. But, I could only know my faith as a child knows it, as adults and leaders instructed me. There is some degree of sentimental attachment to my primal religion and the way it used to be. Sorting through that sentimentality had to be part of my return. I did not want to return for sentimental reasons. We Catholics understand that we are sentimentally attached to our religion, even though it often seems the rest of the world just wishes we would get over it.

We aren't going to get over it. We must educate ourselves and take responsibility for our own spiritual development. I wanted to return to Catholicism for the right reasons—not because I merely like it. I like whiskey, too, but it can kill me if I'm not careful.

What I have in my hand then appears to be conflicting realities.

- I am Catholic and cannot help being Catholic and that is why I am Catholic.
- I must be adult enough to make a decision about whether or not to be Catholic despite some inherent attachment to it.

While I was wrestling with this odd deadlock, a friend of mine converted to Catholicism. He had been raised Lutheran, he was Lutheran to the core of his Minnesota heart. At least that's how it seemed to me. But he had discovered something deeper than his genetic religion. He had fallen in love with the monastic life. He became Catholic; he became a Benedictine monk in a Catholic monastery. His true identity was in the calling he could not help but follow.

That cleared up my confusion. I am grateful to be genetically Catholic. This reality was one I could not escape even as I prepared for ordained ministry in the United Methodist Church. This reality would be with me regardless of whether or not I embraced it. But was I called to be Catholic? Is there something about being Catholic that is crucial to my going to God? Does my soul require that I be Catholic for its health? Yes.

I've talked to hundreds of Catholics about why they are Catholic. Most of us are Catholic by birth. We are not leaving the Church because we have always been, and still are, Catholic. Period. Simple. That's it. The crisis beckons us to consider why we remain Catholic. This is a call to adult faith, a call to responsibility. It was exciting to hear so many Catholics talk of how they are now taking ownership of their spirituality. They have been kicked into action by crisis.

When I started the conversations, I expected disillusionment, anger, even rage. I expected demands that the hierarchy become accountable to the people they serve. And I heard a boatload of all of it. I heard more though. The huge majority of Catholics are not Catholic simply because they can't help it. They are choosing to be Catholic at the point when it takes a whole lot of guts to make that choice. Nine out of ten will not be defecting to the Congregational Church down the road. Not during this crisis, not during the next, not in our lifetime.

We are the generation who learned something crucial from Vatican II. We learned that we can disagree, fight, even dissent, and guess what? No one is going to throw us out of the Church. There are no Catholic bouncers. As long as we keep showing up, the doors remain open and the sacraments will not be denied to us. We do not have to pass through a sensor that will label and reject us as "remarried," "gay," or "dissenter." If we continue to identify ourselves as Catholic, we belong.

Our first experience of this widespread dissent, and the one that changed everything, was the U.S. Catholic laity's response to *Humanae Vitae,* the papal encyclical on birth control. We dissented in huge numbers, with ease of conscience, because the encyclical did not resound of Divine truth. A fully convinced majority of American Catholics said, "Nope, I don't think so." We didn't reject Catholicism, but the laity and local priests knew the hierarchy did not understand married love. They were badly informed.

Vatican II opened a door to change. We could eat meat on Friday. We could visit a Protestant church without permission. We could take Communion without weekly confession; we could take the Body of Christ into our own hands. Women and girls didn't have to wear lace hankies on our heads as a sign of female submission any longer. The priest and altar turned around so that the guy who spoke the Word of God to us was looking us in the eye the way a prophet ought to. Not only that, he was speaking English.

Now think about this. If *those* changes were possible, changes we could not have ever dreamed could happen, just imagine...the monolith was not immovable and unchanging! In the words of the Easter song, "O sons and daughters, let us sing!" Yes, we disagreed but we were not going anywhere. We began the difficult process of growing up as the People of God.

When I was a young teenager, I helped my friend Julie celebrate her fourteenth birthday. It was the year of our first dance party, the year we were allowed to invite boys to the party. I helped Julie plan her party. She was the kind of person who took special care in the details, from the lighting of the backyard patio, to the list and order of songs (we were going for a balance of fast songs and slow boy-girl dance songs), and when the right time would be to grill burgers. There would be many dance parties that year, we were in junior high and back then it was a magical passage into the teen years and adulthood. But this was the first of the parties.

Julie loved Johnny. At sixteen, Johnny seemed much older and so exciting. Much more desirable than the dorky boys our own age. No one could blame Julie for loving Johnny. He was tall with wide shoulders, mysterious brown eyes, and the classic good looks of his Italian ancestry. Julie seemed perfect for him with her long light brown hair, her sparkling blue eyes, and her cheerleader cuteness. People loved Julie, not because she was cute and bubbly, which she was, but because she was kind, relentlessly kind, and she always thought well of people.

Rumor held it that Johnny was on the wild side. The boys thought he was very cool and tough. The girls thought he was vulnerable and exciting, that his wild streak would be tamed by the love of the right girl. His home life was a nightmare. If we had a town drunk, it was Johnny's father.

Julie personally invited Johnny to the party. She called and asked him, "Johnny, would you like to go to my party *with me*?" "With me"—those are the code words that teen-agers understood meant he would be her "date" (not that any of us could date, that was still a couple years away for most of us). Julie and Johnny were friends. He had driven her home a couple times. They had danced at the Valentine Dance the year before. They were together in the halls at school pretty often.

Johnny was Julie's hope for a first and final love. She had already given her heart, God only knows when, and she trusted him with this very important night of her young life.

We were glad for the warm September night since the party was outside. There was magic in the air, we were coming of age with our first choices for who to dance with, who to trust, who to hold on to. Most of us girls expected to lose our hearts that night. It was scary stuff, even at thirteen.

I knew, even before I saw him, the moment Johnny arrived. A wind of anticipation and electricity swept through the place. Anticipation crackled in the music. Now…now the fun would begin. His presence was evidence that we were growing up and we would never be the same after this night. And it's true. We weren't.

I have this picture of Julie in my mind. It was 10:30 in the evening, most of our parents were coming for us at 11 P.M. Mothers would show up in their station wagons and take the budding young adults home to their beds still covered in cowboys and ballerinas.

Julie was dancing; she had turned the music up the loudest it would go. The boy I danced with was the one I would dance with a hundred times. He had taught me how to hit a baseball and I helped him with English and History. We went to church together. Our families were friends. We had liked each other since fourth grade. Securely in the arms of someone who did not even know how to betray anyone, I watched Julie dancing on the patio, dancing alone as silent tears streamed down her face.

Johnny had spent the evening dancing with any, and every other, girl but Julie. Just to show that he was a very cool guy, just because he had the power to break her heart, he did. He made a mockery of her innocent trust and affection. Julie, it seemed obvious to anyone with a speck of sense, had picked the wrong partner.

A lesser soul than Julie would have been inside the house, hiding shamefully. A lesser soul than Julie would thrown a tantrum and embarrassed everyone, including herself. A lesser soul than Julie would have ruined the party for everyone, that magical night of passage, a night like no other. Not Julie.

There in the patio lights, she danced alone and sang to the fading music, "It's my party and I'll cry if I want to, cry if I want to…." She had been violated by this stuck-up, stupid boy, but she was much bigger than him, bigger than his ability to hurt. She would dance while he snickered, it was her party, hers alone. It was her house, her street, her friends, and her birthday. No idiot of a boy was going to drive her off the dance floor.

The memory of Julie came to me one day, not long ago, as I listened to the resignation of Cardinal Law of Boston. I feel a lot like Julie these days. I wonder if I've fallen in love with the wrong one. My trust has been violated. The one I love has spent the night dancing the wrong dance with the wrong partners. The one I love has been out breaking hearts and battering souls—just for the meanness of it. It is certainly enough to keep anyone from dancing. But, like my dear old friend Julie, I am going to stand my ground and keep dancing. I will not be driven from this party in shame. It's my Church and I'll stay if I want to.

What became of Julie? Eight years later she and Johnny
married. They were together for three years. Johnny died in
Vietnam. You would have liked the Johnny that loved Julie.
He could make anyone laugh. He was devoted to his mother.
He loved fishing and kids, Three Dog Night, and motor-
cycles. He loved Julie the way a man who has been brought
back to life loves his savior. He loved her truly, so well, that
it was evident in every exchanged glance and every whisper
between them.

Julie had not been wrong about her Johnny. She saw in
him the strong possibility for love, she sensed something
real and good in him, a greater goodness than the boy of
sixteen had yet chosen. She did not deny that it sometimes
hurt to love someone as complicated as Johnny, with the
baggage of his past and the deep wounds of his childhood.
She never pretended he was anyone other than who he really was; but, she loved him with the conviction that the
goodness in him was the real Johnny.

There is a great goodness in our Church, it has not always been chosen by those we have trusted to lead us, but it
is still there—this gigantic goodness. That is the Church I
have chosen to love, even when it is breaking my heart.

Our Church is still growing up. We are growing. We are all
in process. The Church is not the same as it was a hundred
years ago and will be very different in another hundred years.
Yet, there will be a consistent core to it that remains. It will
change—and it will stay the same.

I have tried to look hard at myself, fearing that this love
of Catholic stuff is an old woman's nostalgia. It isn't, instead
there is something holy in this ancient faith of ours that will
not let me go. It is what brought me home to Catholicism. It

is what keeps me Catholic and what keeps many of us Catholic. I believe that Catholic spirituality holds the most potential to make me fully human. I am Catholic because of the Catholic world-view. Catholic intelligence. Catholic imagination. Catholic monasticism. Catholic identity. Catholic community. Catholic tradition. Catholic unity. Catholic sacramentalism. Catholic joy. I believe, without hesitation, that there is something radically right about Catholicism.

Anti-Catholic religious crusader James McCarthy wrote that he has never talked to a Catholic who remains Catholic because he or she thinks it is inherently "right." Well I do. I've talked to lots of Catholics who do. Come talk to us, Mr. McCarthy. Somewhere at the real center of it all, Catholicism is right.

Greg is a thirty-four-year-old man from New York. He wrote me saying, "I've stayed Catholic because I believe in it. I never remained Catholic because my parents were Catholic or because I thought the bishops always spoke truth. I remain Catholic because it is a life-giving way to be Christian."

Sunny, in her mid forties, lives on the East Coast. She lives a quiet life, taking the homeless into her big old house, one or two families at a time. "Many of my friends tease me that someday they'll find me with my throat cut," she said. "I tell them that being Catholic has taught me that I must risk opening my heart to others. When I feed them, when I offer them a hot shower and a warm bed, I am taking care of God. I am connected to every other human being on the planet because we are all God's children. If there is a single lesson of growing up Catholic that remains with me, it's that one: I am not alone. Pure religion does not allow me to live as if I am."

Choosing Catholicism means choosing to live in community as well. Not that you have to join a monastery or a small-cell group of some sort (not a bad idea though). Ours is simply a desperately and beautifully communal religion. You can be a Lutheran on your own. You can be a Presbyterian all by yourself. They are *sola* religions, me and Jesus got our own thing going. Me and Jesus (and probably *my* Bible) got it all worked out. Well, if I'm Catholic, I don't get to work it out without thinking of others and what the Church says.

Even when I dissent, to remain Catholic means to remain with the difficult thing until the winds of God bring in something new. Change is slow in our faith—but I am glad of it. I have seen too much destruction when change happens haphazardly and quickly. I do not get a personal savior in Catholicism. I will have to make do with the one you have, the one who saves my best friend and my worst enemy. What's more, this mystery of salvation comes to me in the community, through the sacraments, rather than in my own efforts. My own efforts matter, but they will not save me.

David and I have close friends, Tim and Dee-Dee who, as a couple, have backgrounds similar to ours. Tim and I cut our teeth on rosaries, in the same generation, and come from the same kind of brawling, loving, Irish clan. Our spouses grew up Protestant.

I don't recall how it started, but we were talking about Catholicism and Tim said something like this: "What I like about being Catholic is that it isn't about me. Being Catholic means that if I disagree with what's happening in the Church, I don't have the option of leaving because the unity of the

Church is what matters, not my personal opinion. If I think I know something or have insight or revelation, well I just have to wait for everyone else to catch up with me, I don't move on without my brothers and sisters. I don't abandon them. I belong to a family."

I agreed and explained to David and Dee-Dee that this is how it works. Tim and I can disagree on something, let's say women's ordination. We can disagree hotly on it without losing the spiritual reality of unity. How? Well, our opinions are just that, our opinions. And while our opinions are important because each of us is a child of God, opinion is not ultimately what matters. Unity is what matters.

As Catholics we have agreed to abide by authority outside of ourselves. I am not the final say in what happens in the Catholic Church. Abiding by that authority doesn't mean I agree or like it or stop trying to change things. It does mean, however, that I don't walk away. Unity doesn't mean we have to agree. It doesn't even mean we have to like each other. It does mean we are walking under the same banner, and we might have to sacrifice ourselves for what is bigger than either of us.

I can only see one side of the human experience—mine. The view grows wider, when I consider the experience of a whole people. This bigger picture quickly dwarfs my own. Most of us live unrealistically as if our life, what happens in our life, our own experiences do indeed define the limits of God's love. This complete dependence on personal experience as the source of truth is one of our most serious problems if we hope to begin to understand the nature of God and humanity.

Consider the problem of suffering. Without a communal

heart, when I am struck with cancer, when the child I love dies, I am likely to wave my fist at God and demand an answer to the question, "Why me? What have I done to deserve this?"

If I cultivate a life that connects me to others I will soon see that suffering is not the exception, it is the rule. When cancer steals my strength, when death buckles my knees, when loss bends me to the earth, I will lift my eyes to God and ask, "Well, why not me? Why would I be an exception?"

Not only are we communal in the sense that we belong to one another and we look for the higher meaning of being God's family, we are communal in the sense that we believe in a great mysterious thing called the communion of saints. We hold to the belief that those who have gone on before us, who have cut the path for us, who have loved us and are now out of sight—they are only out of sight. They remain with us, they surround us, a great cloud of witnesses and loving support to cheer us as we get out of bed one more time and offer our hand in loving service once more.

Any discussion about Catholic community eventually leads to talking about Tradition. Tradition is an expression of our community. Tradition, with a capital "T" is not the same as traditions. Much of what we have practiced as Catholics is merely tradition, not Tradition. Eating fish on Friday, kneeling at certain points in the Mass, the passing of peace before Eucharist, celibacy for priests, holy water, ringing bells, Latin, all of it is only tradition. We can love it or hate it, it will come and go. It is not the stuff that lasts.

In order that the full and living Gospel might always be preserved in the Church the apostles left bishops as their successors....This living transmission, accomplished in the Holy Spirit, is called Tradition, since it is distinct from Sacred Scripture, though closely connected to it....Tradition is to be distinguished from the various theological, disciplinary, liturgical, or devotional traditions, born in the local churches over time. These are the particular forms, adapted to different places and times, in which the great Tradition is expressed. In the light of Tradition, these traditions can be retained, modified, or even abandoned under the guidance of the Church's magisterium (77–78, 83).

These words are from the *Catechism of the Catholic Church* in Article 2 about the transmission of divine Revelation. What we Catholics call Tradition refers to a living and messy reality that exists only in community. It sounds clean and straightforward, doesn't it? Short version: obey the magisterium. Right. We have bishops who think women should be ordained, we have bishops who think Masses should go back to being said in Latin. Our magisterium struggles to hear God and we struggle with them. Ours is a diverse community in which even the bishops may hotly disagree. Tradition does not prohibit individual conviction. It does however keep me from making a god of my own experience.

Tradition connects us to the past, the people of the past, the culture of the past. Tradition underscores what we must not forget. You may have noticed in poetry, literature, and music that important themes are repeated. If you've read much of the Bible, you've probably noticed something called

Hebrew Parallelism. That means a phrase is repeated for emphasis. For example, "How great are your works, O Lord! Your thoughts are very deep!" from Psalm 92. Both lines are similar in meaning, the second is for emphasis—a very common technique in biblical poetry. This literary device has a purpose—to help us remember whatever it is that we must not forget, and to add the emphasis.

Parents do it too. "Stop right now. Do not go out that door." Lovers do it. "I love you. I will love you forever." It is a very common device for teachers, "Look for the red circle. Do you see the circle that is red?"

Tradition keeps us repeating what we must not forget. Tradition itself would have no power if it were only a dead collection of rituals and dusty rules. Catholicism is a living tradition infused by its ancient rituals with the presence of God and the power of God to renovate the human society and a human heart.

Much of Protestant religion is marked by a repulsion and mistrust of anything that smacks of tradition. The word itself, in some Protestant circles, is cause for sneering. Tradition is considered by these well-meaning folks as obstacles to genuine Christian spirituality. Tradition, and traditions, they would say are created by humans, not God. This kind of talk baffled and upset me when I was Protestant.

In one of the last sermons I heard as a member of Protestant church, the pastor said, "Tradition is what we resort to when we don't have enough faith to do it God's way." Some old startled Catholic part of me wanted to stand up and shout, "Rubbish!" Tradition keeps us on track. Tradition keeps us from building empires with our egos at the center.

Catholics who cherish a pre-Vatican II Church sometimes confuse traditions and Traditions. For example, whether the host is taken in the hand or mouth, whether women's heads are covered when they attend Mass, and even whether celibacy is mandated for priests. Priests have not always been celibate. We've even had married Popes. Many of our traditions are cultural expressions of faith. Some have changed and some will change. The sorting is an ongoing process.

On the other hand, Catholics of a more progressive bent sometimes behave as if Tradition is up for grabs. The Real Presence, for example. This belief can't be done away with and have anything like Catholicism remaining. Take it away and what it means to be Catholic is gone. Take away devotion to Mary—and we might as well be Methodists. Sure, the traditions around Marian devotion get confusing and even absurd, but we can't toss the Mother of God out a window because she's a bit embarrassing right now.

We develop our distinctly Catholic spirituality within the Tradition. How we nurture this sensual spirituality involves some of our traditions. We use rosaries, but you don't have to own a rosary to be Catholic. We use prayer books, but one can be Catholic without it. Most of us do elect to make use of some of these traditions, but it is not required.

Because we live out our Christian faith within a Tradition, we are less likely to fall into the superficial. Ideas about instant gratification are a hard sell on Catholics. Our spirituality as Catholics is shaped by what is classic and enduring. We are naturally drawn to classic spiritual practices such as fixed-hour prayer, meditation, confession, fasting, and service. We incline our ears to hear the voices of the saints that echo from the past, we are more apt to listen to an old idea than a new one—but we don't discount a new idea either.

The spiritual disciplines are one of the ways we claim our faith as adults. These practices assist us in becoming more intentional. Catholic spirituality can quickly fall into the same dangers as any spirituality—paranoia, neurosis, and absolute self-absorption. While we can't, for certain, name a method that will prevent these harmful outcomes, we can do things that will tend to help us be holistically healthy in our spirits.

There is nothing difficult, or unattainable, about the disciplines. And just for the record, the disciplines aren't about severe fasts, lashings, or mutilations such as some "saints" inflicted on themselves. Psychotic disorder does not make for healthy spirituality.

The spiritual disciplines are about having the moxie to say yes to what is life-giving and no to what is harmful.

Because spirituality feels more like gift than effort, it can seem that we are just along for the ride—a rather haphazard approach. There are spiritual practices enabling us to be deliberate about cultivating depth. This deep cultivation of spirituality is something every adult person of faith eventually decides to do, or not.

My friend Judith has been Catholic all her life. I saw her shortly after she returned from a retreat experience, and she was beaming. Naturally, anyone would be pleased for a friend who has found some small spot of peace of mind. I wondered if it would really hold though. In a week, two weeks, in six months, or a year…her retreat experience would not be enough to impart peace of mind.

And, of course, it wasn't. Something really vital had happened on that retreat though. Judith committed herself to "cooperating with God" in her spiritual formation. She started setting aside time every day to pray, she purchased a few books about spirituality, and she started to journal. She told me they seemed like really tiny steps. "I could not imagine how anything so simple could be so powerful."

In the last three years, her husband has been stricken with a disabling illness and she has lost her job. She admits that there have been times when she did not know how she would take one more step.

"And, then, from somewhere, I would feel strong enough to breathe one more time. I realized that those few minutes in silent prayer and the simple attempt to remember God every moment of my life was changing me into someone who could not be rattled, not way down deep," she said. Anyone can do what Judith did. Pray. Read. Sit in the silence and believe that a Voice will speak there. Light a candle. Open your heart to the One who loves you. These actions are how we say "Yes!" to our lives, to our God, and even to being Catholic.

# 4

# It's a Tribal Thing

•◆•

A few days ago Gina turned five. We had a party. Ten kids aged four to six jammed into our living room. I had games planned for the children. I even had a schedule. Adult help was standing by to organize and control the tribe of little ones. I could not have been more prepared.

The first guest arrived, then another, and soon they were arriving in bunches until the house was filled. Quickly I became caught up in the tasks of hanging up coats, lining up boots and mittens, piling sleeping bags (the girls were staying for a slumber party) on the steps, toting gifts to the gift table...and then it hit me, the children, what were the children doing? I pressed through the crowd of adults toward the music.

In the living room the kids were doing something that was not on my schedule. Someone had put on the CD of a very popular children's band. Our little guests were bouncing and bopping all over the living room. The birthday girl was on top of the ottoman doing the twist and twirling in her party dress. Every now and then one of the kids yelled something like, "You go, Birthday Queen Gina!" Who knows what made them think of such a thing?

They did not need organization or planned activities. Put them together, add music, and you have a party. These are kids who go to preschool together, they know one another, they have a sense of belonging. Their freedom to enjoy one another emerges from the sense of belonging.

All of us humans need to belong. During the years I was in a Protestant Church I was reminded, in small ways, hundreds of times that I did not belong. It was never intentional. I just felt out of place, constantly out of place. The path I took back to Catholicism was a path through identity. I had spent my life as a certain kind of person. I was part of a religious group that placed works and activity over being. A person was "saved" they said by faith—and they then proceeded to demand a multitude of actions that would safeguard one's salvation.

Yet, most of them would have fervently denied that they believed in salvation by works. No, salvation by works, that was Catholic, they would have insisted. Still, in that religious sphere, someone was ever laying down rules for the party, setting up an agenda, and insisting that the fate of our eternal souls rested on compliance. It rarely occurred to anyone to simply turn on the music of God and let us dance our way home.

We went to church two or three times a week, tithed 10 percent, spent an hour a day doing devotions and praying. In addition, we were told that we needed to "bring others to

Christ" and we needed to "live holy lives." We were identified by what we did and did not do. We went to church more than our neighbors, we did not participate in the "world" (meaning very little television, no "secular" music or attending movies, no cards, and no drinking). Officially, there was no dancing allowed, but there were always little girls in ballet class, and kids going to prom.

I remember when some of the young girls in the youth group wanted to do a "praise dance" they had learned at summer camp. I was one of their leaders so I went to the pastor to ask for permission. He turned red, pulled at his necktie and said, "W-W-We can't have that. No, we can't. Someone might notice their bodies!" I knew what he meant, but walked away thinking, God forbid that anyone in this congregation remembers that we have bodies.

I want to make it clear that what I'm describing is not what *all* Protestants believe. You're as likely to find a Protestant on the dance floor at a wedding as a Catholic. There is, however, an underbelly to Protestant religion, just as there is an underbelly to Catholicism. Identity happened in that underbelly. It was overwhelmingly a negative identity, but it glued the group together. My Catholicism kept me from ever fitting in. I became notorious as a youth pastor for letting the children dance, sing, paint, and "go wild," as one concerned deacon put it. My Catholicism had taught me that God is among us in the party. This tendency to celebration was part of my Catholic identity.

Identity is one of those words without concrete definition. We use it in various ways, yet the meaning of the word remains abstract. It can mean something as straightforward as name and birth date on your driver's license. It can also mean something as elusive as the qualities that make a person unique. Mostly, though, we know that when we speak of identity we are referring to the mysterious something that makes each of us who we are.

Identity is about being a certain something. It is a remembered thing. Identity grows in a community of family, church, friends, school, work, culture. Some influences are very strong, our families of origin and our first religious experiences are among the most powerful shapers of identity. Our strength, conviction, peace of mind, and our fragile understanding of how we fit into the big magic of it all, this comes from the anchor of remembering who we are.

If I had been paying attention, the fact that I never felt connected to the Protestant tribe would have told me something many years ago. You can spend your entire life trying to sort through what's real and what isn't. Identity, though, has a way of just showing up. It is relentless. It gets you by the throat when you least expect it. We've all had the kinds of days that erode even the strongest heart. Life just keeps coming at us. Identity gets us through times like that.

If you corner me, try to make me feel small, something will rise up inside of me and say, "I am Andrew's and Joyce's daughter, I am the granddaughter of Katherine Starr Collins, the mother of strong young women and grandmother of brilliant and beautiful girls. I am the wife of the finest man I have ever known. My faith has seen me through putting three small caskets into the ground and a multitude of pettiness. I know who I am." Based on this knowing who I am, this knowing that I have been given the grace to endure and to stand where I belong, you won't easily topple me. I'm tough.

You may recall an episode of the TV drama *Chicago Hope* in which the hospital lawyer is shot and Jeffrey Geiger, the best heart surgeon in the country, couldn't save him. The previously arrogant, self-important man whose only identity was his skill as a surgeon quit practicing medicine to raise his goddaughter, saying, "I am not going to be the center of the rest of my life." Identity shifts, enlarges, and takes on the quality of what is most holy when we get over ourselves. It is not strictly about who I am. If it were, we could accurately describe ourselves as a doctor, a teacher, a taxi driver, a nurse, a tradesperson, a singer. What I do matters but it does not define me.

Identity is more about how I am, who I am, how I live as a singer, or how I live as a teacher. Identity addresses questions such as

1. What is my life for?
2. What do I do with my gifts?
3. How do I relate to other people, from the most intimate relationship to the stranger?
4. Where do I belong?
5. To what, or to whom, will I give my best energies and devotion?
6. How will I spend myself?

Without a sense of identity, the experts tell us, we will falter often and most likely feel lost. Catholicism informs our identity. We cannot pin down exactly how that happens, but for us there is no escaping that Catholicism has given us a certain identity.

We have identifying stories. They are God-stories and

human-stories. We are a story-formed people. We live in a culture that is story formed and a community that is story formed. We live out our lives in some greater story than our own, if we are fortunate. There are increasing numbers of people who have settled for living a story that is less than they are, if only because it also costs so little.

Most of us, though, find a story that is so big it is worth living for, and in the context of that story we are shaped, we develop an identity. If this all seems a little abstract to you, think about what you spend your money on, what gets the best of your time, what gets the best of your energy—hidden in there is the truth of whatever story you have adopted and are living for.

Catholic stories tell us about identity. If you grew up Catholic, you have stories like mine. The fact that we both have these stories is part of our identity. Your Lutheran friends do not have the same stories. One of my identifying stories involves my first Communion.

My parents beamed while my grandparents, who were also my godparents, stood next to them. I reached for the large ribbon-topped box on the kitchen table. I was six. What the box contained was no secret—my first Communion dress, veil, and shoes.

After ripping off the ribbon, I unfolded the tissue with great care. When I saw the dress, a lump shaped in my throat, choking out air. I could hardly believe its shimmery snowy beauty or the delicate rustle beneath my fingers when I touched the fabric. I pulled back, afraid to touch it. It was just too perfect for a girl with scraped knees and freckles on her nose.

My grandmother saw my hesitation. She came up behind

me and put her hand on my shoulder. Instantly, she calmed me with her presence. She was an intimidating and strong woman whose ancestors survived the Great Famine in Ireland. It's the kind of thing that puts steel into your genetics. She was also, with me, capable of great tenderness. I don't claim that my grandmother was a tender woman, she was not. She was formidable. As a child it would not have surprised me if she could turn a tornado in the other direction with a single look.

In her thick Irish brogue she said, "It's yours, darling girl, it represents something bigger than any of us and that would be a mighty thing," she stooped, took my shoulders in her rugged hands and turned me to face her. She looked into my eyes and said, "But it belongs to you, and all that goes with it belongs to you. You must wear it with your heart," she tapped my chest, "and with our pride, too. Now, put it on, child, and show us how you shine."

My grandmother, Katherine Starr Collins, of course was not talking only about a dress. She was talking about being Catholic. She was talking of identity. Catholicism is bigger-than-life, it is overwhelming and mighty. If it were less, it would not have the power to build an identity. My Irish grandmother and French mother taught me not to back down from a powerful force. They each taught me to stand up taller when faced with a beast rumbling down on me. Catholicism, perhaps because of its sheer enormity, can cripple a person with its knee-buckling power. It can also teach you to stare right in the eye of the bully without blinking.

A little girl who wears a white first Communion dress and veil, who may see the ceremony surrounding the sacrament as a kind of childish wedding to God, who holds a rosary, who grows up with Mary as the feminine face of the Church, who goes to school with death smudged on her forehead one day every year, that little girl stands no hope of being anything like a nice Baptist girl. Little Protestant girls grow up into a different kind of woman than little Catholic girls do. Not worse, not better, but substantially and obviously different.

The shaping of the Catholic mind begins when we are tiny children. It is no easy thing for a child to be part of something so gargantuan. Identity swirls in the days and nights of our youth and takes on substance as we dust our statues, cross ourselves, have our throats blessed, and clench a medal of Mary during a spelling test. These rituals, the seeds of love for our Tradition, are first dropped into our souls.

I went to Catholic school, and in the winter of my eighth year I learned something about being a girl in my religion. We had religion classes at school. I excelled at them. I was just one of those kids with a head for abstract ideas and so the region of theology was natural for me. This wasn't true of all the kids; the boys seemed especially challenged. Scotty, a boy my own age and friend of my brother, asked if I'd help him with his memorization. I agreed and we worked on it while on the playground after lunch or during recesses and sometimes after school. A couple more boys joined us, and we soon had a study group. These were the same boys I often beat at marbles, the same boys who played baseball in our yard and walked home with my brothers and me. I was a girl with five brothers and very much at ease with boys.

One day after school I was sitting with the boys on a pile of books, reviewing the memory part of the lesson Sister had given us. I was a small child for eight and could easily have been mistaken for five or six. As the boys and I talked, the young priest, associate pastor I think, walked past us. He hesitated, looked at me, and then he turned on his heel and headed toward the school.

A few minutes later the principal came out, she shooed the boys away and asked me to come to her office. She walked ahead of me tall and straight. I remember her face vividly. It was so lined it looked like a map of Indiana. In her office, she asked me to take the seat in front of her. I did. My feet did not touch the floor and I had a hard time seeing over her desk. A few seconds later she came to me, scooped me up into her arms and deposited me on the edge of her desk, then sat next to me. She held my hand for a second, then released it, and smoothed the skirt of her habit.

Without introductory remarks she said, "Father insists that you must stop instructing the boys. He says it is not the place of a little girl. He believes it will make you prideful and give you loose morals." She folded her arms as she stared out the window. There, she had finished the unpleasant, unfair thing she had been told to do.

How is a child to respond to such a thing? I understood pride but was unsure what a loose moral might be. If it were to come loose, I was sure my Daddy could fix it.

Sister shifted her weight and glanced over at me. Then she lifted her tough old hands tenderly to my face, "God willing, it won't always be like this, but for now, you must not teach the boys."

I nodded. One did not ask a principal why or question her, and questioning the priest was even more inconceivable. Sister was clearly upset. I did not understand why. She sighed again, then she said, "You haven't done anything wrong. This isn't a punishment."

I said, "Yes, Sister."

"You may go," she said. I hopped down and headed for the door. As I reached the door she called my name. When I turned she was smiling. She shook her head in that well-what-are-you-going-to-do way that is so familiar to women, and she said, "I hear you beat the boys at marbles."

I smiled back at her and replied, "And Father can't make me stop that can he, Sister?"

Her laughter followed me out of the office. That was a defining moment, a milestone. I have often looked back at that event, understanding now why Sister was so unsettled by the unintentional arrogance of a priest half her age and experience. I knew from that moment on that being a girl was a problem for my Church. I also realized that I had best not let on that I was smarter than most of the boys. It was an identity-forming moment.

One of the things I've often asked of retreatants is that they locate identity-forming moments. Going back as far as memory allows, they consider their lives in five- and ten-year periods, writing out a time line of what was happening in the world and in their families. Then they record personal experiences in the context of the bigger picture, prayerfully looking for moments that shaped the kind of person they have become.

Identity is impossible without memory. I do not create myself new every day. I am the creature of every day of my life and every choice I have ever made. Regardless of my best attempts to live in the moment, I live in the moment surrounded by the breaking waves of yesterday. Identity involves more, though, than simply remembering yesterday.

Identity is about a more unconscious way of remembering. The subtle and unconscious remembering of images and symbols of faith are imprinted on our minds and dramatically shape identity. Catholicism haunts our lives with its ever present abundance of symbolism.

In the early months of my midlife transformation, something was happening under the surface, something I could not name. I caught my first glimpse of it as I became acquainted with Father Pat, the new priest at a local parish. We served together on the board of a local charity. He was the kind of person you liked right away. His wide Irish grin disarmed you immediately and if it didn't the twinkle in his eye was sure to get you.

He rode with me to attend some seminar or another. He asked a lot of questions. I rarely talk much about myself because I'm fiercely private. I surprised myself by telling him the story about the boys, the principal, and the marbles. Something sad inched into his lovely old eyes, he was silent. I've offended him, I thought. Then he spoke.

"I want to apologize to you on behalf of that young priest," he shook his head, "What a misguided soul. I know it's much to ask, but I hope you will forgive us for being so blind for so long." I responded to his gracious apology with a quick internal survey. I could not locate any resentment over the incident— even though I knew his problem with me involved the inescapable fact that I was, of all things, a girl. He did not, in the wide, happy picture of young life, amount to anything. Whatever faith might be, it was not faith in him, I knew that for sure. My family, my faith community, they had never encouraged me to give any priest that kind of power. Our Catholicism was about our family, our life together, where we had come from, and where God would take us. It was our strength in the hard times, the stability of our identity.

These are the kinds of stories that formed the sort of Catholic I became and the sort of person I became as well. We know this much about identity—it gives substance to our lives. Identity brings with it a sense of belonging and pride. The pride is not in self, but in the community and the communal understanding. I am not lost in the many of the Catholic tribe, yet there is always a place for me. I can walk into any Catholic church, anywhere, and I am welcome, I am home. This sense of self creates an inner sort of sturdiness.

In the *Complete Idiot's Guide to Understanding Catholicism,* authors Bob O'Gorman and Mary Faulkner have a chapter titled, "It's a Tribe." I had to smile when I saw the title because that's what my grandmother always called us Catholics—a tribe. I love the image. A tribe lives together, has a common purpose and way of life. A tribe will resist any effort to break it up or separate us from one another, even internal efforts.

Tribal identity has given many of us an unshakable verve, which is rather like guts or grit. Verve is energy, spirit, a kind of inherent strong animation and vitality. Weariness is the opposite of verve. If you were one of the fortunate who saw the first production of "River Dance," you may recall feeling as if something were spilling out of you, something compelling you to weep and laugh at the same time. Irish dance is an expression of verve—a kind of passion. Verve is passion that must do something.

It was 1974, and I was barely out of my teen years. I belonged to an ecumenical group of women that had been formed to address social issues. Two things. First, we thought of ourselves as ecumenical, however we were 99 percent Protestant, Church of Christ, Baptist, Lutheran, Presbyterian, Assemblies of God, Methodist. The other thing I want to point out is that we were not very different from one another. We were all young (under thirty-five), white, and evangelical. Within our various traditions, we were the ones who would have claimed, in the language of the time, a "born-again" experience. We were not all that ecumenical.

Until the day Teresa showed up. She came with Debbie, one of our regulars. Teresa was new in Debbie's neighborhood, the two women had become fast friends. They both had two sons and husbands who worked too many hours. They had both graduated from high school in 1970. But the most interesting thing about Teresa was her Catholicism. She went to Mass each week, carried a prayer book in her purse, prayed the rosary every day.

Abortion was one of the concerns of the era, as were women's rights. We were all against abortion, including Teresa, and in favor of legislating women's rights by means of an amendment to the Constitution. We were considered a little radical by other church women for our stance on that issue. We wrote letters, went to public meetings, began a lecture series at the community center, and were generally taking a safe and sane route toward change.

One night in late November, Teresa showed up at our meeting in a state of indignant rage. It was about Debbie's pastor. He had spent the night in jail after beating his wife and fourteen-year-old daughter. They had both been hospitalized, the wife was released and sent to a safe house, the girl was still in the hospital. Debbie, at that very moment, was at the hospital sitting with the girl and keeping her father away. Debbie's husband was furious that she had become involved in a "man's right to rule in his family."

The deacons had called a meeting and with a single voice announced they would be standing behind their pastor during his time of "family difficulty." They were calling on his wife to return to her marital home and thereby fulfill the will of God for her life. This declaration was all in a statement given to the local newspaper.

Teresa wanted to organize a prayer vigil on the sidewalk outside the church. She had little trouble talking us into it. By nightfall we had our signs calling for the pastor's resignation and repentance in hand. There were sixteen of us, huddled together in our bulky sweaters and jackets, holding candles in our hands, and sitting cross-legged in a tight circle. Teresa sang *Ave Maria* while she wept softly. There were a couple former Catholics, like me, in the group and we joined her song. We sang *Amazing Grace*, and we sang "...and they'll know we are Christians by our love...."

When Teresa suggested we pray the Lord's Prayer together the woman next to me said, in a weary way, "She sure is Catholic." It was midnight and the woman was tired. Even Teresa understood. She wrapped her hand around the crucifix hanging from her neck and nodded, "I sure am." A lump formed in my throat at the tenderness, joy, and obvious pride in Teresa's simple statement.

Catholicism may indeed be responsible for the crushing of many spirits, but it is also responsible for many people of great spirit: Dorothy Day, John F. Kennedy, Mother Teresa,

Thomas Merton, the Catholic priest who gave his life at Ground Zero on September 11, 2001.

Our identity, our tribe, is rich with heroes and thick with verve. We Catholics have overcome monstrous obstacles. We'd like to think that America has moved past its bigotry against Catholicism, however a close analysis of the reaction to the scandal of sexually abusive priests and some members of the hierarchy more concerned with secrecy and power than justice reveals otherwise. One of the most important influences of Catholic identity has been this bigotry. It drives us together, it makes us strong. Our vision of life is countercultural, it is revolutionary. Revolutionists need verve if we need nothing else.

"Historically, Catholics were often not accepted into the larger community and thus gained a sense of belonging by gathering in their parish churches. Although times have changed, the need for belonging remains a strong human desire," writes O'Gorman and Faulkner. The parish is the tribal heart. To speak of leaving it is to talk of leaving home, of abandoning our roots, and even abandoning ourselves.

Those of us who are born Catholic, even when we lose our faith, even when we question our faith, rarely feel at home in any other spiritual homeland. This connectedness has to do with identity. In order to accept another religious environment, there is not only an entire culture to overcome but genetics too. The substance of a Catholic personality is woven from genuflecting and crossing, from the fingering of beads and the scent of incense to prayer cards, Latin chanting, priests dressed in brilliance at the altar, ashes drug across our foreheads, nuns, or at least the memory of nuns.

Our lives were lived in a cycle of churches brightened

by candles and celebration and churches draped in black and darkened as we waited for Light to come among us. In the exhausting short days of December and its seemingly unending darkness, we kneel by a crib and pray for light to find us, to come to us. We light fires at dusk and march the new Light into the Easter Vigil. We kiss the wood of a cross on Good Friday, making peace with suffering and even our own deaths, embracing the hard truth that redemption does not come easy.

I have said previously that as adults we need to choose Catholicism; we need to become more deliberate Catholics. I believe this statement is true. But I also recognize that Catholicism chooses us, it claims us with a loving fury that we will likely never escape. Outside of our Catholic faith there are few who will ever understand the magnetic pull of our religion.

In making a case that my Catholic identity made it impossible for me to be anything else, I am in danger of speaking a contradiction. How can I say I chose it, when it was inescapable? This contradiction is in the realm of mystery. Each of us, someday, in some blessed moment will make the decision to choose life, choose God. Yet, we do so knowing that God initiated the moment, God called us to the moment, and the moment was unavoidable.

I was leading a retreat at the Lutheran retreat house down the road from St. Benedict Monastery when my friend called and said, "Come to Mass today."

For months, I had wrestled, debated, prayed, feeling as if my life would split apart. Everything I knew would be lost the moment I walked through those Catholic doors, for all I knew even my Methodist husband and thoroughly Protestant children would abandon me. I would lose a writing career. I would lose a ministry as retreat leader. There would be no ordination in my future. I had no delusions about it, there was no place in the Evangelical world, or the Catholic world, for a Catholic woman to minister.

But, on that bright July day, when my friend said, "Come," I did not hesitate. Yes, there would be a price and it would get messy, but it was time. I made sure my Protestant retreatants would be in good hands, then I drove the quarter of a mile down the road and turned into a Catholic driveway at a Catholic monastery and went to Catholic Mass for the first time in twenty years.

# 5

# The Catholic Celebration
# of Being Human

• ◆ •

O ne of the great good things in Catholicism is the
affirmation of the human experience. Catholicism is unabashedly positive about humanity.
This conviction emerges from the sacramental mind. Now,
I must admit to wishing that I had other language to express how the Catholic mind works.

David Tracy's much-quoted book, *The Analogical Imagination,* was published more than twenty years ago and it
still serves as the basis for discussion on how Protestant
minds or imaginations are different from Catholic ones.
There's been so much written and spoken on it that I won't
linger on the subject long. It has been popularized by Catholic priest, sociologist, and novelist Andrew Greeley.

On the basis of his work, Tracy suggested that the Catholic
imagination is "analogical" while the Protestant imagination

is "dialectical." What does all of this mean? We Catholics tend to see our lives, our world, our culture, as a sacrament of God that reveals, not perfectly, but still reveals the presence of God among us. The world, for us, is filled with God. It is created by God and good to core.

To the Protestant mind, the world, its people, its objects, and its happenings are obstacles to God, obstacles that must be overcome by endurance and faith. Even one's humanity is an obstacle to be overcome rather than celebrated. I wonder if the phrase, "...I'm only human" was first uttered by a Protestant. I cannot help the mess I am in because I'm only human, I am beastly at heart. Recently, I heard a young Protestant band who does religious music singing, "I am thankful that I'm incapable of doing any good on my own." Catholicism says, "Of course I can do good. God made me and I am, after all, human."

Let me put in a qualifier here. All of this talk about opposing ways of imaging is only about a leaning or tendency. Both ways of thinking are found in all people. They are complementary, not contradictory.

The Catholic leaning is nurtured by the sacraments. This is why Greeley calls the analogical mind "sacramental." I like that terminology, it gets to the heart of it, Catholics have sacramental minds. The person who lives in a world where imagery, metaphor, and symbolism is honored rather than mistrusted becomes a person who hears the more that runs through it all. We do not learn how to locate God in the ordinary by Catholic instruction. Sacramental minds develop because God comes to us in the sacraments, because these means of grace *actually* make happen the thing they represent. Sounds like magic, doesn't it?

The Catholic abundance of symbols and imagery for God create the kind of soul that finds God in every whisper, every drop of rain, every child, every kiss, every breath of every day. All things somehow resemble God. If you want a child to know the presence of God, let him taste that Real Presence week after week. Let her witness and participate in the Holy coming among us in the work of our hands. We Catholics do not remember religious symbolism from the seat of our intellect; we remember it from our souls, from the depth of our God-given humanity. We remember in the way leaves remember to sprout each spring and the way deer seek water at dusk.

When the moment came, this is the way I returned to Catholicism—as if by instinct. The months of struggling became suddenly irrelevant. An invitation to go home had been extended and I found myself ready; after all the struggling, I was ready. My struggles had resolved nothing. Nothing had become less complicated during those months of wrestling with the decision.

I had been playing around the edges of Catholicism, avoiding a decision. I knew that day that it was time to step forward and move into what would come next for me. The whole thing was rather uneventful. I went to Mass, my friend sat next to me. I took Eucharist, I prayed. I went through all the motions rather numbly, just trying to get through that first time. When Mass ended, I walked out of the chapel alone. Father Dan (who would eventually become my writing partner) was out in the hallway, looking like he was waiting for me. I stopped in front of him. He smiled. We were becoming friends by this time.

"I'm happy to see you here," he said.

I nodded, "It's the first time, you know, in a very long time and it all feels rather odd...."

He stopped me from explaining, stopped me from trying to make sense of the moment, instead he hugged me and said gently, "Welcome home."

Welcome. I needed it more than I needed anything at that moment. There would be time to talk later on, time to learn how to be a Catholic three decades after Vatican II. I was uncertain about being accepted as Catholic. I had returned to the church with my history of mistakes and bad choices. Only God knew what lay ahead, but in that moment, I accepted the love of God given to me in the affection of a friend.

The internal turmoil did not cease. I returned to the Protestant retreat place down the road, but I was not the same. The decision was made. First thing Monday morning, I resigned from committees at the United Methodist Church and withdrew my membership. I was Catholic again. Not by birth this time, not by some accident of fate, but because God had called. Believing I had heard this call, I was doing my best to follow. Even though I experienced it as a "calling," for months a cold shiver ran down my spine whenever someone used that word to refer to my decision.

Calling implies that we "hear" God. Hearing is very human, very sensual. Responding to what we experience as a "call" is one way we accept ourselves as humans, one way we celebrate our humanity. The sensual experience of something as simple as affection were the first signs of God's love that I clung to in those days. God in skin—someone that I could hold to. Because Catholicism is positive toward humanity, we expect to know God by our senses, by our humanity.

The traditional five senses are not our only senses. Scientists no longer quibble over this fact—we have other senses. But when we speak of senses we are most often referring to the classic five ones: sight, hearing, taste, smell, and touch. We have now discovered a sense of motion and a sense of light that is something other than vision. We have a sense of listening that is deeper than hearing, an intuitive listening of the soul.

We can also expand our senses with things like stethoscopes, microscopes, hearing aides, glasses, telescopes. We can also take or sense to a world beyond us, a world we may have never seen. We do this by computers, television, radio, movies and we do it with spirituality. Churches take us to a place that is wider than our senses, yet can be known by sensual means.

There have always been movements within Catholicism that are downright hostile toward the body. It's a tough thing to get over. You and I both know it. Our enlightened minds can tell us that our bodies are gifts from God and good, our sexuality is good, our senses are good and can be trusted. But, there's an ancient critical voice countering your hard-found emotional health with reminders of how your body has gotten you into trouble a time or two, as if your body could somehow be separate from you.

When visiting Cincinnati a couple years ago, I went to a cemetery with two other women. I had mentioned to our host that I enjoyed walking in cemeteries. There is something in these places. I feel eternity in them. She insisted that I had to see a particular cemetery. It's a huge cemetery and near the middle of it towers a thickly knotted sycamore tree with gigantic scarred limbs. The twisted massive trunk of the tree is wide enough to carve a small house in it, wide enough to hold a grown woman in the hollow of its trunk.

My Celtic ancestors often used the tree as a sacred symbol—the Tree of Life for example. Jesus used the tree as a symbol of our relationship with God: I am the vine (trunk) and you are the branches, he said. We cannot be separated from one another, that's what he was telling us.

Trees, like cemeteries, speak to me. I have marvelous memories of decorating the tall trees lining the gravel road and driveway of the farm where I lived as a young child. During early summer, when blossoms erupted all over the yard, I would look at those sturdy trees with their dark bark and think how unfair it was that they were so drably arrayed. I spent many afternoons picking wildflowers, even some from my mother's flower garden, so that I could dress those trees in flowers.

There was also a tree in our yard with a tire swing. With a book in my hand, I would rock in that swing for half a day. My brothers often complained that I "hogged" the tire swing, but I just continued to hog it until they went away and eventually it became my swing.

We had a small orchard of apple trees behind the barn. One of them was just the right size for a young girl to climb up and roost in the branches when she needed to escape. I did that many times. Sitting in the tree felt like the safest place in the world. I was free there; no parental nagging to clean my room, no baby brothers smearing grape jelly on my favorite book.

There was another tree. This one was in the woods that bordered my backyard when I was twenty years old. I had just buried my firstborn daughter who had died of cancer at eleven months of age. I was a four months pregnant with the next child. The weather was unseasonably warm for late October in Michigan. The marriage was falling apart, my life was falling apart, and there was no place that felt safe anymore. I would often walk out to the woods, climb into a low-slung old apple tree, pull myself up a couple branches and perch in the nook where the limbs met. It was shaped and sized perfectly for me. It reminded me of the psalm that speaks of being carved in the palm of God's hand.

God seemed very absent in those days. I learned there, in that tree, that it is out of God's absence that God becomes present. There were no simple answers to explain the whirlwind that had swept God from the universe. I discovered that God is not an answer to my worst hurt, God doesn't give answers. God gives himself. In that tree I found myself cradled in the love of God.

I could have never told my Protestant friends that God used a tree to comfort me. That would have been too wacky, new age, pantheistic, and probably too Catholic. Trees, they would have reminded me, are part of nature, and nature is fallen, corrupted, scarred by original sin. They would have not understood a God who met a brokenhearted young woman in an apple tree. God is apt to show up when life gets thoroughly unbearable, and he is likely to show up in some place where you ran to hide.

Anyway, I took to that towering sycamore in Cincinnati. What a delight discovering this ancient symbol for the presence of God in the neatly trimmed and perfectly kept cemetery. It called together every moment I've heard God whisper in the rustling leaf, a young apple blossom, or a sturdy curved trunk. The presence of God seemed to stand guard over the place of lost loves, lost lives, buried hopes, and dreams. The tree's own body and limbs were scarred by etchings made by careless hands. With the passing of time the wounds deepened into the tree, fusing with the tree, becoming part of it, even part of its beauty. I touched the names and dates others had carved into the tree, wondering if we fear death so much that we must scar something as evidence that we have passed this way.

God is scarred by our failures to love and yet stands with us in our places of death, taking whatever pain we inflict and whatever foolishness we hand out. God is among us, healing us, sheltering us.

I leaned into the sycamore, pressing my face into God's shoulder. I had no way to experience the tree other than with my senses. I used my body to get close to it and therefore used my body to get close to God. Of course, the tree isn't God and I knew that. But the image of God it offered to me was very real. I'm Catholic; I have learned throughout the days of my life that ordinary stuff will reveal God to me. It's a small leap from experiencing God in the bread and wine to experiencing God in the wheat and the grape, or even a tree.

A couple weeks later, one of the women who was with me said, "I have a picture of you hugging the tree." She made no attempt to conceal that she considered that a rather bizarre thing for a grown women to do. She had been a little concerned about my reaction to the tree. She is strongly inclined toward the spiritual herself, but her rigid religious upbringing has given her a suspicious view of the sensual, setting it sharply apart from the spiritual. Even though she is introspective enough to know this fact about herself and grow beyond it, she occasionally stumbles into an old pattern.

Using my body to sense God worried my friend. She admitted to me that it did not seem very "orthodox," meaning that it didn't seem like something a Christian would do. Hyperconcern for religious orthodoxy is typical of what keeps us from enjoying a fully sensual life. *Is it safe*, we wonder, *to trust our bodies?* Will our senses lead us off in some wrong direction? In the layers under these questions we find the real question lurking: Can we trust our own humanity?

Jesus spoke with conviction about the importance of loving ourselves, something which seems to have been lost on many spiritual writers. Within Catholicism, this suspicion of the body is sometimes called Jansenism, referring to the particularly idiotic heresy which started in Belgium in the 1600s, spread to France, and then, because Irish priests were often trained in France, to the Irish Catholic culture. Irish Catholicism has powerfully influenced American Catholicism.

Cornelius Jansen, Bishop of Yves, taught that Christ's humanity was not absolute. He believed Christ could not have been completely human and completely sinless because to be human is to sin. Humanity is too flawed to reveal God, that was what Jansen thought: Body? Bad.

Today, the word *Jansenism* is often used to describe what is most rigid in Catholic morality, but especially as it relates to the body and sexuality. Jansenism was not the first theology that considered the body dangerous to spirituality. Gnosticism crept into Christianity early on, set up camp, and stayed around. In this belief system, matter (all of creation) is evil and spirit is good. Matter is never good, it must always be curbed and mistrusted.

Christian spiritualities tainted with Gnosticism and Jansenism abounded well into the twentieth century, determined to smash out any pleasure, bent on suppressing physical love, physical needs, physical expression, physical joy, and anything the body might enjoy—even spiritual delight. This dualism continues to permeate Western culture.

The Christian model of spirituality, though, is Jesus, not some ancient philosophy. Ours is an incarnational way of living. God came to us as a fully human person. This cataclysmic event pronounced humanity as holy, as fit for bearing the image of God—perfectly. Incarnational spirituality requires that we become more comfortable with being human and with having a body. Catholicism does not pronounce our bodies indecent.

I know this is a stretch to believe sometimes. We certainly hear messages from Catholic sources which seem to pronounce us as indecent. These are not genuinely Catholic voices. Catholicism does not condemn us for our humanity; instead, to be human is to have a life teeming with the possibility of knowing God, loving God, and serving God.

Isn't it ironic that a religion based on the belief that God became human should have so much trouble with human bodies, with human senses? Our senses are actually the only means we have of experiencing God. What of our souls or spirits? Aren't these the "place" where we know God?

Perhaps, but when the presence of God snatches your breath away, the moment has been given to you by your senses. You see a sunset, you smell the woods after the rain, you hear a child praying, you taste the wine. Maybe it is the touch of a friend that opens up your soul to receive God. The presence of God is not experienced apart from the body.

Catholicism is serious about the high and holy value of our lives. Catholicism is not cynical about humanity. In an age of derision, we are invited to honor our little lives with greater respect, to trust the way we are made. One of the reasons for this emphasis is that we Catholics take the Incarnation seriously.

The Incarnation is, as the *Catechism* puts it, "...the mystery of the wonderful union of the divine and human natures in the one person of the Word" (the phrase "the Word" is used here as a title, or name for Jesus). You may have heard words from New Testament readings that describe the Incarnation this way, "God became flesh and dwelt among us." I like this rendering of the phrase: "God became human and pitched his tent in our neighborhood."

We've disemboweled ourselves with cynicism about humanity. We are disjointed. We are lost and cut off from ourselves. It's not a new state to the human experience. God comes to the carnage, that's the good news we have called the Gospel. God comes as one of us, as human as you are, as human as I am.

In a moment in time that was unlike any other moment in time, God slipped into the human story in the person of Jesus, son of Mary. He lived as a Jewish carpenter in a Roman-occupied region. A real human, not God dressed up like a human, not God-in-disguise, but a real human. Really God. Really human. My little granddaughter likes to quote Eddie Murphy as the donkey in the movie *Shrek*, "...really, really." God became human. Really, really.

Think about this. The Spinner of the Universe can be contained in the life of one small child who is utterly vulnerable and dependent. Humanity might be broken and has consistently misspent itself, but it is not that far gone if God can become human, if God can come to us as one of us. Humanity is obviously no obstacle to also being divine.

The Incarnation tells us something very important about being human. There is something divine throbbing in our human cells. It is often unchosen, unknown, and even avoided, but it is there, the thumbprint of God on our weary souls. We are better than we know. We are more than we know. We are, for the most part, afraid of becoming all that we are.

Writer Walter Wangerin tells the story of finding the great mountain Denali when he and his wife were visiting Alaska. The story is in his book, *Whole Prayer*. Of course he had expected to find the highest peak in North America easily. How could you miss such a thing?

"Alaskans speak of Denali as though they stood in intimate, awe-full relationship with it. Even at great distance... they can point instinctively toward it—as oriented to the mountain as their own hearts," writes Wangerin. He tells of driving north; north and yet more north—but no Denali. They were able to see mountains, but no Denali.

"We laughed, Thanne and I. We said, 'They're lying. There is no such mountain in Alaska.'"

A few days later, a bush pilot offered to take them into the air to prove the great mountain really existed. So they boarded a tiny red plane and after a while "...the dim rosy shape of a faraway mountain had begun to form in front of us...Denali...the mountain simply swelled before us...there was no earth upon which it stood. I had the strange quality of separation, an unreal air...terrible strength, pure white....I was not loving this titan exultant in its sky. I was fearing it....This mountain was, it seemed to me, autonomous, transcendent, and terrible. Let the Alaskans love it. I couldn't."

God who became one of us, who remains among us, is a gigantic reality that dwarfs everything else. The hugeness of this idea is fearsome if we get close to it. Not because God is so fearsome, but because the holiness of being human, the sacred divine trust that is dropped into our fragile human state, that will take your breath away and change your life. Best avoid it, best deny it, best deny the glory of being human and mock it. Otherwise it will quite literally scare the hell out of you.

Catholicism celebrates the human experience. True Catholic spirituality teaches us to celebrate and enjoy our lives. And to trust the pleasure impulse, to trust our human experience because it is given to us by God. If God can be trusted, then being human must be good. Yes, we Catholics do penance. Yes, we do that whole Lent thing, but not without a party first. A couple years ago my husband and I were on vacation in Nova Scotia (one of our favorite places in the whole world). We were touring by car and came upon a field of scarecrows in Cheticamp along the Cabot Trail.

There are dozens of scarecrows, dressed like hippies, doctors, politicians (the Hillary-Bill Clinton ones were my husband's favorites), priests, firefighters, businesspeople... all of us were represented out in that field as straw people with straw hearts, dressed up in our costumes.

While I snapped pictures of David with the scarecrows, an older couple walked up and the woman asked if I knew

the story of the Field of Scarecrows. I didn't. She said that
during the fourth week of Lent some good Canadian Catholic
farmers said, "I've had enough of this," and they dressed up
in masks and wore the clothing of other occupations. They
went from house to house, laughing, eating and drinking—
during Lent, imagine. They did it in a fashion that was fit
for Lent though, hidden and denying the self. Deny the self,
but celebrate being human; that is the Catholic way.

The Field of Scarecrows, she said, was started by one of
the men who participated in that party, to remind his family,
friends, and neighbors of the occasion. The costumes on
the scarecrows were changed periodically, some scarecrows
were added, some taken away, but always there were some
from the original celebration.

She said, "He keeps it because the tourists love it but
also because he thinks that even during Lent, or the tough
times, we ought to remember the party."

Jesus was often accused of being a party animal. Scripture honestly records the feasts and parties, the shameless
transformation of water into wine. This was a Jesus who
danced with the girls, who teased his mother, who laughed
with his friends at a good joke. When you spot him at the
party, his mouth is wet with wine and the kisses of those he
loved. He was the kind of guy you'd enjoy having over for
burgers and beer. You have to think he would have enjoyed
the Lenten party in Nova Scotia and he would have reminded
us that Lent was created for the good of humanity and not
humanity for the sake of keeping Lent. Deeply ingrained,
even in traditions such as Lent, Catholicism celebrates life
and being human—wonderfully, unapologetically, beautifully human.

Even when we know that God became human and we've experienced our bodies as a gift of God, we struggle. We still seek ways to live on some higher plane, to escape being human. Few of us can comfortably speak of "my body." Hardly anyone can say with joy and ease, "I am a body." Instead we continue to segregate ourselves in dualistic ways. Catholicism calls us to trust God, and also to trust the way we are made.

One of the last things I did in ministry in a Protestant church was lead a support group for those recovering from serious dysfunction in their families of origin. The people who gathered each week looked very emotionally healthy. They held good jobs and raised families. They were, without exception, wonderful people with a world of magic alive inside of them—all of it mostly unknown to themselves.

It was someone's forty-fifth birthday that night. A few of us met to buy him a drink after our meeting. There were a couple of gifts, black balloons, you know how it goes. One of the women raised her glass to the man as our celebration wound down and she said, "Happy Birthday; just think, you've been a disappointment to your mother for almost half a century."

A shadow of pain crossed his face, then landed in his eyes for a second before he laughed, and the others began laughing. I finished my wine wondering if any of us will ever know just how wonderful we really are.

# 6

# For What It Is

•◆•

R obert Frost wrote, "We love the things we love for what they are." I cannot love Catholicism for what it is not. God knows, I am painfully aware of what it is not. But I do love it for what it is. Being Catholic is like being in a family. This similarity is obvious to other Catholics—maybe because our families are also Catholic.

Like my church, my family has made mistakes, sometimes holding on to ideas, even ideas about ourselves, that we should have released a long time ago. Theories of child-rearing are one example. My parents and their parents considered it their high duty and obligation as parents to provide for us, make sure we had food, warm beds, and leakless roofs over our heads. They also strived to make us responsible people who would follow the rules.

They were a responsible group themselves who would sacrifice anything to provide for their children and who expected, in return, obedience and loyalty. There is nothing wrong with obedience and loyalty—but the words fall on our ears with definite discomfort. I remember when David and I were dating and talking about marriage he asked me to think about what it was I wanted in a husband. I did not have to think about it. I wanted loyalty. He replied that maybe I did not want a husband, I wanted a dog.

Obedience and loyalty are not enough in relationships. Children are not tomatoes that grow correctly if tended correctly. Many of my parent's generation did not understand that you have to honor a child's deep dream. They didn't know the joy of spending hours playing with dollhouses and trucks or finger painting in the shade of big old tree. They rarely built sandcastles, they hardly ever taught a little girl how to catch a ball. They seldom had time to rock a sleepy-eyed child. It was hard to raise a family, one had to be practical and teach children to be practical. Few of their generation ever listened to the first song a child sang, or honored the first page he colored. Too many gifts of dandelions were greeted with "There are bugs in that," as it was tossed out the door.

Well, yes, there are bugs in it. There are bugs in everything. God flung into being a world whirling and crackling with complexity, a world filled with bugs. It is also a world thick with beauty, jammed with goodness. It is all very good. Still there will always be bugs in the flowers. Until we accept the bugginess of it all, we will not accept the creepy-crawly things in our own hearts and—in our Church.

Not long ago, I was reading reviews posted on the book site Amazon for a Catholic book. Most of the reviews were thought out and fair, if not completely positive, at least fair.

Then I found one that accused the author of "perpetrating the Catholic myth," and being overly attached to his own naive and sentimental view of Catholicism. The reviewer seethed because the author wrote with "warmth" toward the Catholic Church. How dare he!

If you accused a Jewish person of being overly attached to her Jewish identity we'd suggest that you are a bigot, Madam. Catholics, however, should feel shame because our Church is imperfect? Well, why shouldn't Methodists feel ashamed? Or Anglicans? Or Lutherans. Open your eyes; there are occasional devils in clergy collars and robes everywhere. Why would an adult even expect otherwise?

Get a clue. Perfection does not exist in the human experience. My own children cut their teeth on this basic principle. Mom is not perfect; they learned that fact young. Dad is not perfect. We love you, we try hard, we do our best, but we will fail you at times. Our lives are beyond describing with all their glory, but they are also pitted with a pox that inches in on our everyday living.

Organizations, institutions, churches, these are made up of people who bring with them the baggage of their neurosis, their wounds, and their faults. Whatever is managed by people will be capable of both great good and great evil.

A friend of mine is a religion writer at a major daily newspaper that has covered the sex-abuse scandal in the Catholic Church. She has been swimming in the details.

"I'm so weary from the darkness of all the failure and all the pain that my joints hurt," she told me. "I'm a reasonable and intelligent woman. I know nothing is perfect, but this is just so damned imperfect. Sometimes I go home and cry for all of us."

David Yount, Quaker, syndicated columnist, and author of *Be Strong and Courageous*, said that he tends to "think like a Catholic" even though he isn't. "I think Catholics should hold on to the very much that is good in your Church and get rid of the rascals."

One of the reasons there are rascals and villains in our Church is that the people in the pew just never paid much attention to those guys. I corresponded with a lot of Catholics while working on this book. If there is anything they agreed upon, it was that the hierarchy of the Church had been far removed from the concerns of their ordinary daily lives long before the scandal arose. In the words of a man who is studying to be a deacon, some Catholics consider Church leaders to be "...puffed with [a] sense of their own power and living in a world of their own."

Gen, a Catholic women living in Michigan said, "Ultimately, our faith and belief, that is Catholic, is not centered on these men. We believe what we believe because we consider this as the way to find God. If we looked up to priests, who are mere mortals, as the *reason* for our faith, we'd be way off base and frequently disappointed."

"My faith is not based on anything any priest or bishop does," wrote a Catholic man from Florida who will soon be eighty-five years old. "Never has been, that hasn't changed. I stay Catholic because it's where I find the strength to keep going. I learned how to be a Christian in the Catholic Church. If I do say so myself I'm pretty good at being a Christian."

The common message, the one running through all the interviews, e-mails, and discussion was this: Catholicism is not perfect, and this imperfection is not even news. Nothing is perfect, why would religion be an exception? Faith can only be based on what is, on what holds, on what is real. Faith based on anything else is sure to crumble.

One priest told me that a parishioner came to him speaking of how "disillusioned" she was and how "disillusioned" other people were. "I understand her pain, but I look at it this way. If someone is believing in an illusion it should be dissed."

Karen, in her forties, is a Catholic woman living near Seattle. However, she grew up near Boston, an originating point for the recent sex-abuse scandal. "You know, whispers about inappropriate sexual activity involving priests have been around for as long as I can remember," she said. "I recall going to my mother when I was maybe seventeen, and asking if she had heard the rumors about Father so-and-so. I asked if that was the reason he had left the parish. Mom looked down at her dishes, she said something about the church leaders taking care of it. She said it was not our place to question or judge.

"It was not only bishops who looked the other way. Catholics in the pew did it too. We did not want our comfy world toppled by the truth. The other day I reminded Mom, who is now seventy-four, of that incident. She shook her head, denied it hotly, and said she would never have justified such a thing."

We Catholics have been pointing our fingers at some of the hierarchy. But, hey, where were we when this was happening? Yes, there was a prevailing "Father Knows Best" mentality before Vatican II, but I know of hardly a Catholic who still adhered to it in 1973. Instead, what some Catholics have told me is that they most often simply gave scant attention to the guy in the collar. He was needed for the sacraments that define Catholic life, but he was not otherwise a "major player" in their lives. Did Father ever get to be human? Did anyone think of his loneliness? How often did someone look past the collar to the human being?

Often I write with a collaborator who is also a priest, Daniel Homan, OSB. He told me a story once of celebrating the first Communion of a bunch of kids in a parish where he served. Every family wanted a picture of him with their child. As he was finishing up with all the photo-taking, someone's grandmother said, "Father, it must make you happy to be in so many family albums."

"That night was the loneliest night of my life," he remembers. Yes, so many family albums, but never his own family album, his own children, his own wife. As the families went home to celebrate, their good and beloved priest ate dinner alone.

No matter how much you might wish for perfectionism if you've reached adulthood, that dream is no more than an illusion. Why can't we get rid of the expectation?

Maybe because the yearning for perfection, for something that is so holy is inviolable, is an indication of some bigger reality. Maybe our souls, carved from the essence of God, remember the grand peaceful wholeness of divinity, and so we chase it down all the days of our lives.

It's so easy to expect perfectionism in a Church where talk of authority and infallibility are common. The Church does not claim to be perfect though. Under the loud, rushing currents of infallibility and hyper-authoritarianism are the rocks of reality. These are the rocks that have held up Catholicism for two thousand years.

" 'The Church on earth is endowed already with a sanctity that is real though imperfect.' In her members perfect holiness is something yet to be acquired" (*Catechism of the Catholic Church,* §825). Real though imperfect, here we are with what seems like another contradiction. When you hit a contradiction like this one you can be sure that you've come to the realm of the sacred. Jesus said you live to die, the first will be last...contradictions all.

There is a Holy Reality within Catholicism. It is the undeniable substance that holds us together despite the evil among us. When I felt exiled from Catholicism in my Protestant world, I caught a glimpse of it and that's what called me back.

In his book *Callings,* Gregg Levoy tells the story of marine animals north of the Inside Passage along the Alaskan coastline that are trapped in a 34-mile-long "lake" created by an ice dam. The seals, sea lions, porpoises, and such are expected to die of starvation. Eventually, though, the ice dam collapses, violently and unexpectedly. It frees the trapped and dying animals, sweeping them to freedom in the tidal collapse. "Sometimes, a collapse is the only way to freedom," writes Levoy.

What Levoy says is a profound and important spiritual principle. Life comes from death, it rises from the ashes like the ancient Phoenix story and the resurrection story. This rising from the ashes is part of the Hercules myth. The relentless story we tell over and over again is of how Good will somehow emerge from the biggest Evil we can conjure up. It is a universal reality and, while it might make us shudder, we all know that it is true.

By celebrating what is good in Catholicism, I make peace

with it. I make peace with who I am. I make peace with my family. I make peace with God. It is in places like churches and families that we learn how to belong to a diverse, irritating group—just like real life. We learn in the family, and we learn in the Church, that humanity contains great and good souls and a few evil ones too. We learn tolerance, we learn how not to hold a grudge, and if we have been anything like well-loved we learn how to forgive.

Who we are becoming happens on the bright wings of our memory. Remember who you are and from where you came and you stretch forward. Remember and you belong. Memory is how Catholicism has shaped us and it is how it holds us. Somewhere in that tangle is the sacramental magic that is worth it all.

My journey home to Catholicism is littered with sacramental magic, like the chance encounter with an near-stranger. One afternoon, I went to the post office and ran into a woman I barely knew. We had met a few times, no more. She stopped me and started talking. She had recently been on retreat at a tiny Lutheran monastery nearby. She had been searching for peace of mind in a complicated time. It must be like that for me, with my daughter's accident, she continued.

"I'm not sure why I'm telling you this. I think it would be good for you," she said. She wrote the number down on the back of her card and pressed it into my hand.

I wanted to go directly to the monastery. I wanted to run like hell in the other direction. I told my husband about it that night and he suggested that maybe a few days away would do me good. Something seemed to be cornering me lately. It took a week for me to conjure up the nerve to call.

"Have you ever been to the monastery before," the guest master asked.

"No," I admitted.

"Do you know why you want to come?"

"No," I said again, if this was a quiz I was failing.

"Well, then. I will give you our nicest room. Can you come next week?"

"Next week," I found my voice, "But, well, that's so soon."

"You might as well get to it," he replied with a chuckle in his voice.

*Indeed*, I thought, *I might as well*. It was the next step, I was certain. Something waited for me there that would take me onward. Feelings and fears were crashing around inside of me like a ten-car pileup. Some wiser part of me with eyes wide open already knew the direction of this path. It was like being sucked in by gravity—or maybe by Love. I could only follow and try to believe that the confluence of these events was pushing me forward. I had no guarantee that it was. I only knew that my inner life of indecision had become unbearable.

And how bad could the timing be? Andrea was still recovering from her accident. Our older daughter, Shelly, had just gone off to college and was away from home for the first time in her nineteen years. What a year it had been. Still, can you come next week, he had asked. Yes, I said. Yes, I will come.

Astronomy experts were predicting that a few nights later we would be able to see shooting stars. When that night arrived, I was still in turmoil. Shelly called to remind us to go outside about midnight and look up. She would be doing the same thing. Shelly has been, still is, the appointed keeper of family unity. She holds us together when we would otherwise come apart and that night she reminded us once again that even though distance separated us, family cannot be separated, not really.

I wasn't sure about the whole star-gazing idea. I watched Andrea limping as she hauled out binoculars, sleeping bags, pillows. Why subject ourselves to the elements, I wondered, on the half-hope that we might spot some light streaking in the sky. Why tolerate the damp air, Michigan mosquitoes, and sleeplessness for the remote possibility of a few shooting stars?

I could not say no after the phone call, after watching Andrea dig out supplies. She had a pile going on the porch. I expected her to get out the beef jerky and bottled water next. To her, it was an adventure. How does a teenaged girl who has nearly had the life knocked out of her make an adventure of a Wednesday night under the stars?

"Don't expect too much, Honey," I said to the girl who was walking after a few months, walking when the chances of it had been declared to be "remote" at best. I reminded her that the best sightings were expected to be on the East Coast.

The screen door at the back of the house banged. My husband had ducked out. I glanced at the clock, 11:45 P.M. The enchanted hour was upon us. Andrea and I followed, our arms stuffed with the supplies he had not been able to carry. We plopped them down next to David's pile as he said, "I don't see anything."

*Isn't that swell*, I thought. I glanced at Andrea wishing I could keep her disappointment away. Resenting the night sky because it has refused this brave child the spectacular light show she hoped for.

"They said you might not be able to see it without binoculars," she reminded him.

I don't recall how long we three stood there under the stars, not sure what we were looking for, what it would look like, if we would even know a shooting star when we saw one.

Into the dark stillness Andrea spoke, "I saw one."

David glanced at me and shrugged.

"It was probably an airplane, Andrea," I said.

"I know a star when I see one, Mother," she muttered in teenaged girl fashion.

I turned my gaze to the corner of the sky she was watching. Within seconds, something streaked brightly across the black canvas. It happened so quickly that I was left blinking and wondering if I had seen what I thought I saw. But it had left glowing red dots in my eyes. Andrea was right. When you see a star, you know it.

"There's another," I said, pointing.

We kept looking up and, as we did, we stepped backward, eventually we were out on the golf course behind our home, watching a sky that seemed to roll on forever. I was the first to unroll a sleeping bag and stretch out. Then Andrea, finally David. We lay very still, all heaped up together in a family lump. We discovered that only by watching one small area of the sky very intently could we see the shooting stars. We had to resist the urge to let our eyes wander.

Change was in the wind. I wanted to hold this night for my family, frozen in time. It seemed as if we had called the lights from the sky to witness to the huge pain in our family.

That night, though, we were somehow together, even across the distance, watching breathlessly as the sky danced for us. We were together looking hard, keeping still, witnesses to the enchantment of the universe. It was a moment when light broke into our quiet suffering and we pointed to the light, we called one another toward it, and we held our breaths for the holiness of it all. We were, under those stars, in the whole thing together as change charged at us.

One late afternoon, a few days later I drove up a long winding road toward the little monastery. I knew that a quarter of a mile down the road was a Catholic monastery. I passed the place I was going to be staying, and drove down to the Catholic monastery, turned, and slowly inched up the driveway. I could see the bell towers, I could see the retreat house; across the lawn a man made long strides, his black habit slapping against his ankles. He didn't slow down when he saw my car, but he did glance in my direction and that was enough to make me back up and head for the Lutheran place. This Catholic place, it was still too scary. I wasn't ready, nope, not ready.

How could I know that place would eventually become my spiritual home, the one place on earth where my weary heart would finally come to peace? God was inching me toward it, slowly. For now, I headed for cover at the Protestant place down the road. I arrived and trudged toward the guesthouse where the guest master met me. I put the monk out of my mind. I would not think of anything Catholic.

I followed the guest master down a corridor, listening to his directions, accepting a schedule. He swung the door open and I stepped into a small bedroom, obviously decorated

for a woman. I glanced around, wondering what I was doing here.

The monk continued to provide helpful instructions as
I followed him into the room. He stopped abruptly and
asked, "Do you like beer?"

I turned to look at him. "Beer?" This was too weird.

"Dark beer. German beer. Roll-out-the-barrel. You know.
Beer," he was smiling.

I had not drank any beer after becoming a Protestant.
Beer. There had always been beer around at our family parties as I grew up. Beer at the Communion parties, the con-
firmation parties, the weddings, the funerals. For my family
Jesus would have changed the water into beer.

"Well...yes," I said. Yes. Why not. "I think I'm quite
fond of beer." I smiled.

"Excellent then. Tonight we have friends visiting. He
brews beer. She is making cheesecake. I am going to make
popcorn. You're welcome to join us in the family room. I
think we might watch a movie," he paused. "I suppose you
came to pray."

I didn't know. None of it was making any sense to me.
Perhaps I had come to this odd little monastery to drink
beer. Certainly spending the evening drinking beer with
strangers and eating popcorn was not how I imagined my
first night in a monastery would go, even if it was not exactly a Catholic monastery. I had no agenda. So, I joined in
the beer-drinking and conversation. Later we prayed night
prayers together. I slept soundly, even missing early prayers
the next day.

Eucharist was a bit later in the morning. Someone
showed me the right place in the book and I settled in, still

sleepy, but more relaxed than I had felt in a very long time. There were no expectations of me. No one monitoring whether or not I was doing serious spiritual work. I could drink beer and take a nap without anyone fussing over it. My guard was down—that's how God got me.

Eucharist began and I could not take my eyes off the chalice in the hands of the celebrant. My throat cracked with thirst for the cup as the symphony of an ancient and familiar liturgy brushed away the brittle parts of my dried out heart. *What is he doing?* I wondered, *this is the Catholic Mass, this isn't Protestant!* Lutherans, I soon learned, have a rite that is very much like the Roman one. It was like spiritual bait-and-switch.

Uncontrollable tears streamed down my face. I was not sobbing, not even really crying, there were just rivers running out of me from some long-ignored reality that would no longer be silenced.

The absurdity of it was that I had been taking communion for more than two decades as a Protestant—and this place was Protestant. It was not as if I had gone without Communion. But this cup was in the hands of man dressed in priestly garb and the liturgy was indiscernible from a Catholic one. Never had a cup seemed to bend to my broken places and pour life into the cracks. This was a coming to my senses and facing something undeniable about myself. I am Catholic. To deny it is to deny myself.

The body of Christ broken, the blood of Christ spilled. It is scandalous how literally we Catholics take this Eucharist of ours. I knew a woman who went to a Protestant church that did not allow "negative talking." She boasted that all the songs were only positive, there would no singing of

"Amazing grace...that saved a wretch...." She likes this church, she said, "...because people are so cruel, life is a jungle." She liked communion there because they did not talk of broken bodies and flowing blood. She did not have to look at a corpse on a cross. Instead, they received "...a token of God's presence among us."

You can't really blame her for wanting relief from the jungle, can you? Church should be a safe place, a shelter, right? We hope it will be safe, we work together for the day when churches will always be safe for the vulnerable.

Faith, however, must find ways to address the certainty that you can round a corner and meet a semi, head-on, through no fault of your own. Faith cannot ignore the hard reality that melts your bones and makes you dizzy. Awful things happen sometimes. It seems random, like being swallowed up by the sidewalk. So we go to church as we are, strangers to one another, strangers to ourselves, exiles in a place that seldom makes sense and often rips the heart out of us. We don't know how we have gotten lost, but we arrive at the door of the church assured of our own lostness and hoping beyond hope that we will get found.

How sad to arrive in such a state and have to tolerate cheerful ditties and motivational speakers. My Catholic soul shudders at the thought that rather than having the cracked places in us salved with the Body and the Blood of Christ, we get a yellow ribbon tied around the wound as a "token of God's presence." There are so many lies, so much phoniness—why would we want more of it at church? Give it to me straight, Father. Give us a burning bush and the thunder of a prophet, but please don't make us pretend, not in church.

In Eucharist, God is present in the suffering. No, it doesn't hurt less because of it, but mysteriously, the awful thing is tolerable when God is with me. God has not inflicted some horror on me, God is not a sadistic monster who enjoys my pain. This is the image in the Eucharist that holds me together: God suffers with me. God is not distant from the thing that smells like burning flesh.

The celebrant placed the cup in my hands, his hands covering mine. His eyes searched my face with a touch of concern. We held the cup together, for a second or two, as I steadied myself and then he let go, bidding me to take and drink. In that moment, I remembered who I am and where I come from. As I took the bread, and the wine burned a track down my throat, I was dazzled by the clearing of my head and calming of my heart. How had I survived without this?

I returned the cup to him. He didn't know whether to smile or weep with me. He gave a slight nod as if to say, "Well, all right then," and moved on to the next person in line. I felt like skipping.

In that not-exactly Catholic monastery, I engaged with my Catholic inheritance for the first time in two decades. I had given up the richness of my own language, imagery, and faith. I had given up the power and peace of my identity. I had excommunicated my own soul. There in that chapel I was very close to going home; I was well on my way. In Eucharist we meet our ghostly, faded selves, our Doppelgängers. It is blood and body that we need or we fade away completely. With the cup in my hand, I remembered. I turned toward home. I turned toward truth. Keeping us true, this is the work of what is best in all that is Catholic.

Remember the Robert Frost quote? "We love the things we love for what they are." I suspect it isn't exactly true. We fall in love with what we love for what we think they are. It is very rare to fall in love without blinders. This innocent ignorance can only take you so far though. Eventually, you have to face the facts; eventually, there's a tough reality to be handled. We remain in love for what our lovers really are, and for what they can become, and if it is a mature love, we even remain in love for the sake of what is lacking.

The bigger good in Catholicism is so big. There is a whole lot that is right about our faith. There are many, many reasons beyond what I've talked about for loving Catholicism and for remaining Catholic. The Catholic story is strewn with error and even evil. So is the human story. This existence of evil and error does not keep the magic of loving and life from happening; even the random sadness doesn't keep joy from bearing down upon us. Catholicism is good. It is very good. One of the most important reasons that I believe Catholicism is good is that it does not require my smile when my heart is broken. It does not require a prettified cross without a body on it. It does not require cheerful ditties on Sunday morning. Catholicism is good because it allows the truth to be told.

Art is one of the ways that Catholicism tells the truth. I love the fact that so many artists, musicians, and film producers have Catholic minds. Not just Michelangelo, but Bob Seger too. We don't get to claim Mother Teresa without claiming Madonna. They startle, challenge, enrich, and shock us, out of those wild Catholic imaginations. Imaginations that were not smothered young.

I remember the summer I taught at Vacation Bible School.

I was in my early twenties with a young child. My seven- and eight-year-old charges were scattered across the back- yard of the church, beneath the sun, some beneath the trees, all of them painting on large sheets of paper. They did not have easels. Sitting cross-legged like wise old sages, or bent earnestly over their papers, they were, each and every one of them, engrossed in the work of painting Creation—our Vacation Bible School theme.

As they painted, periodically their perfectly shaped little heads would tip up from their work and scan the sky, a tree, maybe the kid a few feet away, or even the church parking lot. It was hard to tell if they were actually looking at any- thing or just trying to remember something barely out of mind. It astonished me that when children of that age were given a can of paint and a brush they could be happily oc- cupied.

The day was growing hotter and so we encouraged the children to finish, clean their brushes, and then take their creations into the air-conditioned classrooms.

I knelt next to Rachel and put my hand on her shoulder, "It's almost time to go inside," I said.

She turned toward me, leaned back on her legs, still kneeling, and said, "That's okay, I think I'm done anyway."

The children had done wonderful work. Lots of green grass, bright flowers, bugs, dogs, fish, bright sunshine, even a few lakes, mountains, and tigers could be found. Obvi- ously none of them felt restricted to paint only what was in the church yard. We had not told them to go out and paint the church yard after all, but to paint Creation.

Rachel's painting, however, looked as if it had never even seen the church yard. You could tell the sky from the grass, but suspended between air and ground was a swirl of color with eruptions of yellow, orange, and red. I thought it was rather Van Gogh-ish. I liked it very much and complimented her. She asked if I would carry it while she cleaned up (she was a bit of a painted mess herself) and I agreed, heading toward the door with painting in hand as Rachel wandered over to the buckets of soap and water.

One of the older women, Diane, who was instructing an older age group saw the painting in my hand and stopped me. She asked if she could look closer. I handed it to her saying, "Isn't it remarkable?"

She looked at it for a couple of seconds and then shoved it back at me, as if repulsed by the thing.

"I guess you could call it that. She didn't follow instructions though, did she? Part of training children in the way of the Lord is that they take instruction."

"Diane, she's just a little girl and we told her to paint Creation. She did that."

"She had to use her imagination, what is on that page is not what she was looking at, at least not in this world. It looks, I don't know," her voice dropped, "possessed."

My Irish temper was about to rupture.

"There is nothing wrong with imagination," I replied.

"Well, no, not within limits. You know, a Christian imagination. That thing is something else. What do you think she was looking at? That," she pointed to the paper, "is clearly beyond the limits of acceptable imagination."

It was my first encounter with an usually unspoken suspicion of imagination. A suspicion I did not encounter in my Catholic education. Catholic artists and writers have long tried to give voice to the movement of salvation among us, the uprising of God to take over our puny kingdoms and make Kingdom Come out of them.

Jesus is the poet and storyteller who is the model for Catholic language and imagination. He said the real thing is like yeast in bread, or a pearl you discover in the field one day when you're pulling up weeds, or the silver medal that your grandfather gave you when you were four and is so precious that when you lose it, you turn the house on its end to find it. The kingdom comes to us as the most precious thing in the world that somehow we lost, and it shows up behind the toilet just when we thought it would never be found. That's the kind of stories Jesus told. He engaged the human imagination. In Catholic ranks, imagination and creativity is deeply honored.

I realize that some Catholics have had a bad experience with Sister who would not let them paint the tree purple and that there are Protestants who understand the deep worth of imagination. But, speaking generally, and on admittedly treacherous ground, Catholicism tends to be less cynical of imagination.

How does it happen? There is the bounty of symbolism in all things Catholic. We end up back there again. The way Catholics internalize symbolism uses imagination. This internalization isn't the same as seeing things that are imaginary. Imagination is the ability to make the abstract real. We need it to believe in love, we need it to believe in peace, we need it to believe in the stock market.

The most logical among us have trouble pointing to reality, imagination helps us locate and express it. Physicists have long held that time and space are not absolute realities. At speeds close to the speed of light, time seems to slow down, and space, some say, starts shriveling and shrinking. Quantum physics has shown us that some subatomic particles have what they call a "nonlocal" quality. This means they can communicate with particles that aren't local, that are separated by long distances. They are mysteriously connected to those particles.

Well-known Quantum Physicist David Bohm has speculated that this is what accounts for how twins know when each other has been hurt or is troubled. Bohm says there is an "implicate order" in which everything is part of everything else. Okay. Now, try to understand that without a little imagination.

Catholic imagination has given us great art, great science, and a world of beauty. A religion making use of such an enormous number of symbols is bound to birth enormously creative souls. This abundance of creative souls is one of the great goods in Catholicism that has enriched the human experience, not just the Catholic experience.

Attempting to articulate what *is* in Catholicism rather than what is *not* is a little like trying to explain what makes a piece of music powerful or takes away your breath in a sunset. When I consider what Catholicism is, rather than what it is not, it makes me a little dizzy with all of its goodness. When I let myself be open to what is good and life-giving in my faith, the terror of what needs reforming loses its power to strangle the joy out of Catholicism.

# 7

# It's a Whole New World

•◆•

I returned to Catholicism like a pilgrim returning to a homeland after a long, long absence. Not only had I changed, the Catholic Church had changed while I was away. My head was full of questions. How would I be Catholic again? What had I learned as a Protestant that would help me be a better Catholic? What would I do to serve in the Church? Opportunities in Catholicism would be few.

Within weeks of returning it became clear. I was different from most Catholics. My years as a Protestant were the reason. I was a woman with a formal education in theology. Among Protestant laity I had known many people who, even without the formal education, studied Scripture, were interested in it, read books on spirituality. The people I was meeting, they were wonderful people but only the monks had theological training. I was becoming friends with the monks, but my relationships among the laity remained very

121

casual. These were not people I would see at the Wednesday night Bible study.

Even with this awareness, I did not feel compelled to do
anything about it. Life had stripped and stilled me. In the
hours I spent walking the monastery grounds, praying with
the monks, or just sitting in the chapel, it ceased to matter
if I was like the others I went to church with. I dropped my
expectations of them and I dropped the expectations of
myself. I had encountered a whole new world, and my old
sets of expectations were no longer going to work.

Suddenly, stilled to the very center of those ego patterns
I had been avoiding getting to know, I saw how I had shaped
a life with a relentless fury for finding out more, a continual
hunt for the deeper meaning, and, always, ever in my consciousness was the drive to "be someone God can use." Sitting in the monastery chapel I realized that I did not want
to be someone God could use, not anymore. I just wanted
to be someone who could let God love her.

The theology of activity, doing, going from one good
thing to the next, this "doing of salvation" was the first Protestant layer I shed. I had done it all in the name of working
for the Gospel and working for God. This kind of effort can
wear the bones paperthin. I had learned no spirituality of
waiting and waiting, I knew instinctively, what was required.
Whatever I might eventually grow into as a Catholic person
of faith, wherever the next path lay, it would not be found
by more activity.

How would I create an inner sanctuary strong enough
to hold me during the uncertainty of waiting? Was there
anything I had gained in those decades as Protestant with
enough substance to get me through the waiting? Not only

through it, but into whatever came next. During this time I looked into a program at a nearby Jesuit institution that trained spiritual directors. A retired Jesuit priest showed me the facility, then we had coffee in the cafeteria.

He asked if I felt a calling to be a spiritual director. I began to laugh. I don't think it was the first time the gracious priest had ever seen someone crumble into hysterical giggles at the question because he calmly stirred cream into his coffee and waited while I regained my sanity.

The word *calling* rang empty to me, I explained. In the name of calling I had seen people do heartless, cold, and cruel things. In the name of calling, I had witnessed people herd up on opposite sides to do battle. In the name of "calling" and "God's will," I had seen one too many acts that ranged from simple stupidity to intentional viciousness. I wanted no act of mine to labeled with the word *calling*.

This deep conviction left me without a way to talk about, or even think through, what I felt. I had once talked of a calling. A calling to write. A calling to ministry. A calling to serve. It was all gone now, faded into the past along with my attempts to be Protestant. My struggles to make sense of it were compounded by the failing of my religious language. I told him that I felt as if I had been on a fast train toward some sort of spiritual goal or achievement and now I was derailed. I told him that I was glad about the derailment, it was time to get off that train, but now I had to get myself back on track toward some kind of spiritual formation.

He nodded. "Don't be so quick to put yourself back on the train. Perhaps waiting, resting by the side of the tracks is exactly what you should be doing. He reminded me that the will of God is not a goal I pursue, it is the place where I wake to find myself. It is the path at my feet more often than it is the fork in the road.

I'd been impressed by how many Catholic mystics stressed an interior knowing of God. God is not outside of us, giving instructions like a third-base coach. God is inside, an inner guide. What if I looked inside, waited and rested in the God within rather than chasing after some outward noise? Thomas Merton said of the Interior Guide, "We don't have to rush after it. It was there all the time, and if we give it time, it will make itself known to us."

Lent began during this time. As the priest rubbed ashes on my head, he whispered, "Dust to dust...." The ashes were a sign to me of the waiting period I had entered. I would need to live without answers. I would need to live without images for God. I had been awaking, for many months, to a growing emptiness and a muffled interior noise, as if something in my depths were weeping. Something unvoiced, something silenced for too long. It was the clamoring of the real self, refusing to be denied and ignored any longer. The change-winds that had taken me home to Catholicism were moving me onward, to something I could not see, something new, something frightening.

Change-winds are also swirling through our world and our Church. The cold of it can penetrate us the way December rain does. Outside the cabin where I write a December rain falls. It is icing over the winter-stripped limbs of trees and the scattering of snow around my cabin. For a little while this afternoon, I sat out on the porch that runs the length of the log cabin. December darkness fell fast and hard tonight. By 5 P.M., it was upon me and the cold came with it. Out on the porch I was wrapped in two heavy blankets and drank a cup of hot black coffee laced heavily with good Irish whiskey. No matter, nothing could stave off the cold. For so long, I have felt nothing but a depleting, baffling ache in my soul. That's why I stayed out in the cold even when I could no longer feel my toes inside heavy wool socks. The exterior numbness reflected what I feel. My Catholic soul needed the imagery.

The cause of this acute aching? Not just one thing, but many piled up one after another. The sorts of things we all deal with: illness, career shifts, moves and changes, disappointments and betrayals. Through the upheavals I discover not only that others will let me down, not only that there are so few people who are what they seem to be, I discover that I am very far from being what I seem to be too.

This personal crisis of mine, it is running parallel with what is happening in our culture and our Church as one after another monoliths are proven to be pitted thoroughly with failings.

Ultimately, this emptiness or upheaval, however we name the crisis, it calls us to come home to ourselves. I know that now, ten years after returning to Catholicism, it was a call, I no longer shudder at the sound of the word. In the turmoil, we are called home.

I have always had a rather wintered soul, more at ease in the stripped frozen plains of a hacked off winter day than the balmy long days of summer. So I am familiar with a deep kind of sadness and know that it is not the opposite of joy. I am not afraid of the winter rains and winds of change any more.

I will stay in the Catholic Church for much the same reason that I stayed on the porch tonight. I was there to be a witness to the icy rain. I was wrapped up snug to watch the coming darkness. I am a presence, a witness. I stand here with my single lighted candle against the night. It will not ward off the darkness, but neither will my light be extinguished. And the lights of each of us, all of us Catholics who aren't going anywhere, together we can drive out the darkness, if we just vigilantly keep the light burning.

Tonight I woke up, suddenly and totally, about 2 A.M., thinking of a friend who has had a tough time for a few months now. I made a cup of hot chocolate and went to one of the big upstairs windows in this cabin. I looked out. The sterling glow of the full moon had transformed the frigid winter night into a thing of beauty while I slept. Across the surreal looking snowy landscape, the moon shadow of the trees streaked like vivid black cracks, sharp in the silvery night. I stood at the window transfixed. There is a beauty to winter.

When we were talking a couple days ago my friend described himself as in the "winter of life." Looking out the window, I could see that the beauty of winter is harder to appreciate than the beauty of, say, spring. But it is still breathtaking. Winter strips the trees, revealing everything, allowing nothing to hide. Winter reveals the strength of the tree. Trees in Michigan seem vulnerable to bugs, pestilence, and the elements for the rest of the year. The stripped trees of winter seem fixed and strong. You shiver for them, pray for them, but you so much envy the courage and fortitude hidden by the softer light of summer.

Catholicism is in a wintry kind of season, not because it is dying, it certainly is not, but because it has been stripped and now stands alone in the cold. Nothing will remain hidden. Terrifying, isn't it?

But we are also able to see the strength, the endurance, the shape of the real thing that is present and holding us all together. It is not, just as Catholics all over America have told me, the priests or bishops who hold the Catholic Church together. Let us love them, let us serve them, let us help them…but let us rise up and remember who we are. We are what holds our Church together. This Church is ours. This faith is ours. It has come to us from the lands of our grandparents and it has come to us through our own adult choices. It is ours.

When my oldest daughter, Shelly, was six, she started having severe pains in her legs and feet. After a battery of tests and a thorough examination the pediatrician said she was having "growing pains." I thought my mother made up that term. Every night, after her bath, I would rub her legs and feet with lotion, warmed in my hands as she lay on her back, propping one foot at a time up on my shoulder while I tried to ease her pain. That and a little Tylenol™ seemed to do the trick.

Except that one night when it didn't work. A night that I stayed up with her, read *Cinderella* to her countless times, braided and unbraided her long hair, sang her favorite songs and rubbed her legs until she fell asleep, curled up next to me in front of the warmth of the fireplace.

In the morning, as she slept on the couch, I prepared her favorite breakfast of apple spice oatmeal and "dipping eggs" (over easy). As I cooked, she tore around the corner of the kitchen and stopped right in front of me, drew herself up straight and said, "Look, Mommy, I'm finished growing."

She would happily stay six-year-old size if it meant she

did not have to hurt anymore. Anything to bypass a night like the one we had just had.

To grow up as a people of God, to grow as a person, a couple, a family...in all the ways we human beings become more than we are right now, we suffer growing pain. Our beloved Church is writhing with it right now. What has happened to our ability to live with the ache? When did we determine that spirituality and profound living would be without price? When did we start clutching at the formulas and ten-step solutions rather than remaining with the Divine Mystery that can transform us?

Having returned to Catholicism, I still don't know where I fit or if I will ever fit. The strongest sense of belonging I have comes when I sit in the chapel at the monastery, or I listen to one of the monks tell a joke. The strongest sense of belonging happens when I dance with my grandchildren, when I lay in my husband's arms, when one of my children tells me something they have never told another soul. The strongest sense of belonging I know, that is what I feel when I share a meal with a friend, and when I take a walk in the woods.

Protestantism taught me to look for belonging in the institutional church, in the religious system. I tried to make that work as a Catholic and it didn't—it could not. Catholicism calls me to belong to a wider world, to the people who love me, to a community that reaches beyond the walls of my personal cloister. My vision of faith and life, it is being stretched by the Catholic faith, and conversion happens in this stretching. I have not enjoyed the growing pains.

When I was a very young girl, maybe five, I used to spend hours drawing. I just loved it. One of my favorite things to draw was nuns. I would cut them out, making them into paper dolls. I had dozens of them. Under the tables and chairs of the dining room I created a Catholic world. My nuns scurried around the floor at our house, going from one adventure to another. They saved lives in Africa and China, they started hospitals and defeated bullies. They held great big parties where dozens of other paper dolls danced and sang. My little nuns were a lively lot.

I was so young to know the truth about Catholicism. It is an adventure, and lives are saved and bullies defeated. There is a great big party. This is Catholic joy. It cannot be bullied, beaten, or threatened into silence. We will not be defined by those who are evil, ill, and desperate among us.

We find in this great Catholic faith not simply a cultural way of life, we find not a mere communal experience. Look beyond the creative urge, the rites, the ancient liturgies and see what is beating at the heart of it—our Living God.

You would not, today, be a Catholic unless you've been overwhelmed by the brightness of it at one time or another. God is the brightness of our faith. God is the keeper of our faith. In the words of the endless Catholic liturgy: Thanks be to God!

God, the one we look for in all the symbols, God the one we are missing in every ache of loneliness, the one we love in every kiss. God who has been at the center of our faith from the beginning, God who will remain with us. God who will, somehow, manage to save us and our Church. God who bears us up. God who loves us into the promise of whatever it might mean to be Catholic for one more day. Thanks be to God.

# Resources

•◆•

These are books and Web sites that I have found useful in personal spiritual formation and cultivating a better understanding of contemporary Catholicism. I hope you may find something useful here.

## Books

*Awed to Heaven, Rooted in Earth, Prayers of Walter Brueggemann*, Fortress Press, 2003.

*The Catholic Youth Bible*, NRSV Catholic Edition, St. Mary's Press, 1998.

*Desire of the Everlasting Hills*, Thomas Cahill, Doubleday, 1999.

*The Good News According to Luke*, Richard Rohr, Crossroad, 1997.

*The Sacred Journey: A Memoir of Early Days*, Frederick Buechner, Harper Collins, 1982.

*Godstories: New Narratives from Sacred Texts*, H. Stephen Shoemaker, Judson Press, 1998.

*How to Keep a Spiritual Journal*, Ronald Klug, Augsburg, 1993.

*Catholicism* (New Edition), Richard P. McBrien, HarperSan Francisco, 1994.

*Letters from the Holy Ground*, Loretta Ross-Gotta, Sheed & Ward, 2000.

*The New Jerusalem Bible: Saints Devotional Edition*, Introductions, Selections and Commentary by Bert Ghezzi, Doubleday, 2002.

*The Path of Life*, Cyprian Smith, OSB, Ampleforth Abbey Press, 1995.

*People's Companion to the Breviary* (2 volumes), Carmelite Monastery, Indiana, 1997.

*The Rule of St. Benedict*, translated by Leonard Doyle, Liturgical Press, 2001.

*Monastic Practices*, Charles Cummings, OCSO, Cistercian Publications, 1986.

*Soul Feast: An Invitation to the Christian Spiritual Life*, Marjorie J. Thompson, John Knox Press, 1995.

*What Makes Us Catholic*, Thomas H. Groome, HarperSan Francisco, 2002.

*Why You Can Disagree and Remain a Faithful Catholic*, Philip Kaufman, Crossroad, 1995.

## Journals, Magazines, Annual Publications

*Magnificat*, a little journal containing the daily office in a prayer format that anyone can easily follow, published monthly, yearly subscriptions. *www.magnificat.net* or 301-853-6600.

*At Home in the Word*, Liturgy Training Publications, annual publication that has brief commentary and reflection on the Sunday readings.

*Daily Prayer* (2003 is the current issue, but it is published yearly); Liturgy Training, annual publication with a straightforward and simple format for daily prayer.

## Web Sites

*www.osb.org*. This is the official Web site for the Benedictine order. It contains links to all things Catholic, plus lots of other links. I think it is among the best of the Web. The one Web site I would hate to do without.

*www.universalis.com*. Daily prayer is available here to read on your computer or download to a handheld device. Very good directions, easy to navigate. Excellent site.

*www.catholicnewworld.com*. This is the newspaper for the Archdiocese of Chicago. There are many excellent Catholic publications but this is the one I read most often online.

*www.liguori.org*. Web site for information, ordering books, and so on.

*www.paracletepress.com*. Another excellent publisher that sells books, has study guides and articles. Very nicely done.

# About the Author

·◆·

Lonni Collins Pratt is also the coauthor of the award-winning books *Benedict's Way: An Ancient Monk's Insights for a Balanced Life* and *Radical Hospitality: Benedict's Way of Love*. She has received numerous journalism and writing awards during her career as a newspaper and magazine writer. She is also the author of several other books about faith and spirituality. She lives in rural Michigan.